"Veronica Litt is an excellent movie night companion.
Reading *Ugh! As If!* feels like settling in for a post-
screening conversation with a witty, warm, and feminist
friend who knows a lot about gender, class, and race, but
also about rom-coms, Jane Austen, and ditzy teen heroines.
*Ugh! As If!* makes a powerful argument for why we should
keep inviting Amy Heckerling's film into our lives, and it
reminds us of comedy's awesome power to connect us."
— Deidre Lynch, author of
*Loving Literature: A Cultural History*

"Litt's lively, original *Ugh! As If!* works like a rose-
colored kaleidoscope, using the brilliant teen movie
*Clueless* as a lens to examine the broader cultural
landscape. With playfulness and depth, she makes a
case for a more thoughtful approach to "feminine"
art, shedding light on everything from the scourge of
cinematic status anxiety to the nature of love."
— Emily Nussbaum, author of *Cue the Sun!*

"For women's media to move forward, we require serious
inquiry into art that not only highlights the difficulties of
womanhood, but the light, humorous, and fun. Litt gives

*Clueless* the intellectual importance it deserves, adding it to the canon of timeless women-led pictures."
— Marlowe Granados, author of *Happy Hour*

"Just like *Clueless*, *Ugh! As If!* is an unabashed celebration of all things girly, bubbly, and bright. Through a combination of film history, critical analysis, and interactive quizzes that will warm your *Seventeen*-magazine-reading heart, Veronica Litt shows us that this ditz-forward teen movie is ultimately a story about how we can become better people by living within and learning from community. If you've been feeling jaded about the state of the world, this sweet, smart, and funny book is exactly what you need."
— Hannah McGregor, author of
*Clever Girl* and *A Sentimental Education*

# the pop classics series

# ugh!
# as if!
# clueless

## veronica
## litt

ecwpress

Published by ECW Press
665 Gerrard St. East
Toronto, Ontario, Canada M4M 1Y2
416-694-3348 / info@ecwpress.com

Editor for the press: Jen Sookfong Lee
Copy editor: Kenna Barnes
Cover and text design: David Gee

Library and Archives Canada Cataloguing in
Publication

Title: Ugh! As if! : Clueless / Veronica Litt.

Names: Litt, Veronica, author.

Series: Pop classic series ; #15.

Description: Series statement: Pop classics ; 15 |
Includes bibliographical references.

Identifiers: Canadiana (print) 20250140667 |
Canadiana (ebook) 20250140683

ISBN 978-1-77041-816-5 (softcover)
ISBN 978-1-77852-404-2 (ePub)
ISBN 978-1-77852-405-9 (PDF)

Subjects: LCSH: Austen, Jane, 1775–1817—Film
adaptations. | LCSH: Heckerling, Amy—Criticism
and interpretation. | LCSH: Clueless (Motion picture)

Classification: LCC PN1997.C58 L58 2025 |
DDC 791.43/72—dc23

Printing: Friesens     5  4  3  2  1
PRINTED AND BOUND IN CANADA

This book is funded in part by the Government of Canada. Ce livre est financé en partie par le
gouvernement du Canada. We acknowledge the support of the Canada Council for the Arts. Nous
remercions le Conseil des arts du Canada de son soutien. We acknowledge the funding support of
the Ontario Arts Council (OAC), an agency of the Government of Ontario. We also acknowledge the
support of the Government of Ontario through the Ontario Book Publishing Tax Credit, and through
Ontario Creates.

Purchase the print edition and
receive the ebook free. For details,
go to ecwpress.com/ebook.

For my big sister, Shannon

# Contents

## Ugh! As If!: Introduction

The screen is drenched in ultramarine blue. Playful *whoosh*es, *squeak*s, and *boing*s erupt like fireworks. Bold, chunky letters in fuchsia pink, butter yellow, and neon green declare that Paramount Pictures presents: *Clueless*. With a snappy drum lick, we transition to the "real" world. A loqued-out Jeep carries tittering teenage girls dressed as brightly as birds of paradise. A smiling blonde preens with three large shopping bags. She prances down a crowded high school hallway, laughing with her stunning best friend. She frolics at a pool party and flirts with a handsome waiter. The montage slows down as she flips her perfect hair and announces, "So, okay, you're probably going, 'Is this like a Noxzema commercial or what?' But seriously, I actually have a way normal life for a teenage girl." She's lying. Her life is nowhere near normal. But it's okay — this world is beautiful and bright. We can spend 90 minutes basking in this girl's blissful existence.

The fairy tale world of *Clueless* (1995) revolves around Cher Horowitz (Alicia Silverstone), an obscenely wealthy, beautiful, and self-obsessed sophomore at Bronson Alcott High School.[1] Cher is used to breezing through life — her otherwise gruff father is wrapped around her finger, she leads the in-crowd at school, and her bottomless bank account disqualifies any money woes — until her (admittedly small) problems pile up and force Cher to reckon with herself and her place in the world. As she grapples with mediocre grades, a nightmarish driving test, and truckloads of her own interpersonal incompetence, Cher slowly but surely learns to be a more considerate person. With the heroine's metamorphosis complete, the movie ends when Cher and her friends attend a joyous wedding. General Public's sacred bop "Tenderness" plays and the credits roll. Everyone lives happily ever after, perhaps including the viewer. With its sharp script, big-hearted message, and charming performances, *Clueless* is the perfect feel-good movie.

When Amy Heckerling first shopped *Clueless* around in the early 1990s, teen comedies were not seen as a bankable genre. If a movie was set in high school, chances are it was a heavy drama about hardship (*Boyz n the Hood* [1991], *School Ties* [1992],

---

1 Fun fact: The high school is named after Bronson Alcott, an education reformer, lovable dingbat, and, most importantly, father of Louisa May Alcott, who wrote *Little Women* (1868–1869).

*Above the Rim* [1994], *The Basketball Diaries* [1995], etc.), so studios weren't exactly chomping at the bit for lighthearted fare like *Clueless*. Add to this the fact that *Clueless* was an off-the-wall adaptation of *Emma*, an 1815 novel of manners by Jane Austen, and Heckerling had quite the hard sell. Even so, Paramount Pictures eventually took on the script, perhaps remembering that Heckerling had directed another hit high school comedy: *Fast Times at Ridgemont High* (1982). Of course, this turned out to be an excellent business decision. By the end of 1995, *Clueless* was a certified success.

Reviews were mostly positive, which, to this day, is unusual for a high school comedy (not exactly a critical darling, that genre). *The New York Times*'s Janet Maslin called Alicia Silverstone a "delectable teen queen" in one of many raves celebrating her sparkling lead performance. Heckerling's linguistic brilliance and whip-smart script also received near-universal praise. Sweet, good baby Roger Ebert wrote that *Clueless*'s dialogue "could be anthologized."[2] On the other hand, the film's ambiguous treatment of materialism didn't go over so well — *Rolling Stone*'s Peter Travers thought it was as frightening as the hopelessness in the bummer drama *Kids*, written by Harmony Korine and released the same year. And of course, a few critics incorrectly dismissed the entire movie as inane drivel. Writing for *Entertainment Weekly*, Owen Gleiberman characterized *Clueless* as "marshmallow fluff."

---

2 I love Roger Ebert. He was the rare film critic who could appreciate popcorn movies like *Anaconda* (1997), *Charlie's Angels: Full Throttle* (2003), *The Mummy* (1999), and *Never Been Kissed* (1999). He correctly gave *Clueless* three and a half stars out of four.

Audiences, though, responded warmly. The movie made bank during its theatrical run, earning over $50 million in Canada and the U.S. (and that's 1990s money). This meant *Clueless* more than quadrupled its production budget. Released on VHS in December of 1995, *Clueless* then became one of the most popular video rentals in America. Appealing to a relatively neglected fanbase of teenage girls and young women, Heckerling's Rodeo Drive *Emma* quickly spawned a series of young adult books, a three-season TV show based on Cher's continued adventures, and a certified-gold soundtrack album that holds up to this day. Fans of the TV show could also buy unhinged tie-in merch like a CD-ROM game where you raided Cher's closet and gave avatars makeovers, a digital organizer with a calendar called "Wassup? Mode," and a landline phone with buttons that played catchphrases from the movie (naturally, one declared "As if!"). Where Heckerling mined rap music, slang dictionaries, and Los Angeles high schoolers for the film's dialect, her script in turn shaped the way real teens spoke. "I'm Audi" (I'm outta here), "surfing the crimson wave" (having your period), "keepin' it real" (not being a poser), and "whatever" (with little W hand symbol, natch) were all coined or popularized by the movie. *Clueless* was a pop cultural juggernaut.

In the years since its initial release, the *Clueless* train has continued to gain steam. Now a beloved '90s classic, the film's enthusiastic pop cultural afterlives include endless yellow plaid outfits in qualities ranging from polyester Spirit Halloween costumes to expensive high fashion. I thrifted the former in a

Value Village, while Donatella Versace produced the latter in her Fall 2018 collection, leading to *Clueless* revivals at other fashion houses. Natalie Portman and Tessa Thompson wore Dior and Oscar de la Renta while channelling Cher and Dionne (Stacey Dash) at a press junket in 2022. Photoshoots and glitzy events constantly feature stars recreating the movie's sublime/demented costumes — Beyoncé, Bella Hadid, Naomie Harris, Olivia Rodrigo, Amanda Seyfried, Willow Smith, Harry Styles, and Taylor Swift have all been snapped in extravagant *Clueless*-coded outfits. To help the rest of us achieve the look, a Silicon Valley tech company created a real version of Cher's virtual outfit simulator in 2021.

Across social media, film, and TV, *Clueless* continues to make waves. The glossy Hindi rom-com *Aisha* (2010) intertwined both *Emma* and *Clueless*, suggesting that Heckerling's film holds as much cultural capital as Austen's canonical novel. The music video for Iggy Azalea and Charli XCX's massive hit song "Fancy" (2014) referenced *Clueless* scenes in debate class, the freeway, and the party in the Valley. The self-aware teen movie *Do Revenge* (2022) tipped its hat to Heckerling's film via preppy costumes, snappy dialogue, and a major location named Horowitz Hall. Remakes and reboots are regularly pitched by Hollywood executives — over the years, projects including a riff by the writer of *Girls Trip* (2017) and a potential TV series revolving around Dionne have made headlines (before descending into development hell). Alicia Silverstone constantly references her trademark role as Cher in social media posts, a Super Bowl commercial, and fashion campaigns.

Gen Z star Dove Cameron starred in an off-Broadway musical version of the film in 2018. A West End musical came out in 2025. And, perhaps the greatest sign of an adaptation's success for me as a lifelong Austen fan, even the Janeites are on board. The latest major film adaptation of the text — Autumn de Wilde's delightful *Emma* (2020) — paid homage to *Clueless* in its theatrical release poster. Anya Taylor-Joy's Emma wears a Regency gown and feathery hat in the exact same shade of yellow as Cher's signature outfit.

The steady stream of homages confirms it. We are still majorly, totally, butt-crazy in love with *Clueless*. Even 30 years after it hit theaters, *Clueless* keeps us coming back for more. But why? We have heaps of charming '90s teen movies. What's so special about *Clueless*? For me, the answer lies in the film's most iconic quotation: "As if!"

First, the words "as if" ask us to imagine what could be. Those four letters contain entire worlds beyond our imperfect reality. They're wishful, dreamy, hopeful, enchanted, open-ended. They're optimistic. They're a lot like the movie *Clueless*, which sees our protagonist, Cher Horowitz (who easily stands in for the rich and powerful), pivot from an oblivious ding dong to a well-intentioned community builder. In the beginning of the film, Cher expects a blissful life; at the end of the film, she's learned to work for that better life — both for herself and others. Cher's transformation is a powerful reminder that all is not lost, that even the most unlikely people can change for the better. The film suggests that if the 1% could fail their driving test, have an epiphany at a fountain, "makeover [their] soul," and take tangible actions to rebalance social inequity, we might end up in a more caring, compassionate, and joyful society.

I'm sure that all sounds nice, but if you're anything like me, you may also be feeling like you overdosed on sap. Enter: the second meaning of "as if." This phrase also expresses a cynical disbelief that such goodness could ever come to pass. Those two words are like a curtain dividing the real-world audience from the fantastical "happily ever after" onscreen. To hear the possibility of goodness and respond with a curt "as if" — it extinguishes faith, it doubts decency. And honestly, fair enough. The world is so terrible so much of the time. Cynicism seems inevitable. But as Cher's progression reminds us, giving in to despair and pessimism will do us no good. If we don't like the world that surrounds us, accepting its shittiness as unchangeable will shift the dial zero degrees. Maintaining hope is necessary.

It's this dialectical toggle between optimism and jadedness that characterizes *Clueless* and its everlasting appeal. This satiric, sweet movie imagines a lighter, kinder, better version of the world with enough bite and self-awareness that even the most skeptical viewer can be nudged into feeling emboldened about the future. It's possible to recognize problems and think constructively about amending them without plummeting into complete doom-and-gloom pessimism. All this leads us to the film's ultimate thesis: *Clueless* argues that idealism is more useful than cynicism, that hope is more powerful than despair, and that community is more valuable than isolation.

At its best, *Clueless* makes this point through complex treatments of femininity, love, and connection. But, as in most movies, Heckerling's argument emerges in uneven fits and starts. Some sections of *Clueless* perfectly support the thesis that we can improve by fostering community and cultivating compassion. Other scenes and plotlines contradict Heckerling's rosy message. *Clueless* is very much a product of its time (the 1990s), while also containing baggage from its source text's time (the 1810s). As a result, some of the movie's ideas and arguments have not aged well. Heckerling sometimes over-romanticizes Cher's innocence (even when it pivots into ignorance) and endorses her heroine's skewed perspective in the movie's limited treatments of class and race. These are dicey elements of the film and I'm not going to bother excusing or defending them. Instead, I'll examine them.

Tackling the movie's thorniest elements means examining the story's internal logic and seeing where idealistic messaging falters or breaks entirely. Since *Clueless*'s avowed message is all about making the world better, these stress points are productive places to push on. They represent social problems that the film doesn't address in a satisfying way, like the limitations of the rich ditz character, why it's not a great idea to wholesale lift plotlines from bygone centuries, and the oh-so-1990s notion that we can solve racism through color-blindness.[3] To truly

---

3 Chapter five, "Not to Your Face: Friendship and Silence," is all about this. Go in prepared to channel that bewildered Larry David gif.

learn from this movie, we need to consider its most effective elements as well as its pitfalls.

I would like to see this story continue, because despite its occasional fumbles, I love this film. When everything seems hopeless and passivity paralysis takes hold, *Clueless* energizes viewers into believing that we're not doomed. With enough optimism, good-heartedness, and commitment to doing the work, we can change things for the better. I mean, what else are we supposed to do — give up and let inequity, selfishness, and injustice rule the day? As Cher would say, "Ugh! As if!"

# 1

## Total Betty: Feminine Art

Stereotypically feminine art doesn't have a great reputation. For decades, pop music, romantic comedies, Harlequin novels, and other genres that cater to women have been accused of being juvenile, escapist, and formulaic, among other aesthetic sins. Even when critics admit that certain pieces of girly art is good (as with *Clueless*) or when contrarian op-eds champion the artistic merit of reality TV or soap operas, media created for femme audiences still faces an uphill battle. Movies and TV shows like *Barb and Star Go to Vista Del Mar* (2021) and *Sex and the City* (1998-2004) are still not considered legitimate art and definitely not in the way that Oscar-bait dramas are seen as significant films about the human condition. This is why girly media is often called a "guilty pleasure." As a rule, we aren't supposed to admit that we like this stuff. If you do, you embarrass yourself. You out yourself as unsophisticated, as unserious, as less than your peers.

I still remember an icebreaker from fourth grade. The teacher asked the class about our favorite movies and, in order to look cool, everyone cited the most violent, intense, serious movie they'd seen. I claimed *The Terminator* (1984) was my favorite, which was a huge lie, but I wanted to fit in. Everyone else was saying stuff like *The Matrix* (1999), or *Twister* (1996), or *Titanic* (1997), which back then was risqué and mature because it showed boob and made you cry. I don't want to speak for everyone because, hey, maybe some of those ten-year-old children really did love those dour, scary movies.[4] But I remember what my friends and I actually watched on movie night — *Beauty and the Beast* (1991), *It Takes Two* (1995), *The Parent Trap* (1998) — and that wasn't it.

I think a lot of us already knew at ten years old that there were some things that were "deep" and "cool" and okay to like. On the other side, there was stuff like *Spice World* (1997; popular and fun, but for your little sister), *Ever After* (1998; amazing, obviously, but unmentionable in front of a boy you liked), and *Miss Congeniality* (2000), which we had all seen and loved but which only one girl — of course, the unpopular girl — admitted was her favorite movie. The lesson was clear: You couldn't ally yourself with that kind of thing. It would

---

4 My angelic, absurd sister, Shannon, may have been one of these kids. She had a poster for *Titanic* hanging in her room for years. During a *The Craft*–influenced Wicca phase, she used it to cover up a pentacle she put on the wall with glow-in-the-dark paint. For me, this act encapsulates girlhood in the 1990s.

be social suicide. Better to play along and pretend Arnold Schwarzenegger didn't haunt your nightmares for months on end.

Over the years, I've done a full 180 on this attitude. I've come to see girly art from a different perspective and I genuinely respect, appreciate, and admire how rom-coms and pop songs counter some of our culture's most pernicious and deeply held ideas about what is worth our time, effort, and attention. Sparkly girly movies like *Clueless* can share joy, hopefully depict social progress, and encourage viewers to exercise their emotional muscles. Maybe most importantly, they can bring us together. Something can only be classified as pop culture if it achieves a certain level of popularity, if it's supported by a sizable audience. The people need to form a kind of consensus and collectively agree to give something our attention. Popular art thus takes individuals and turns them into a community united by our shared love of a film. Obviously, a monoculture is not an automatic cure-all for ever-increasing political polarization and the vagaries of neoliberal individualism, but under certain circumstances and with certain kinds of shared art, I think considering and celebrating films like *Clueless* can help more than hinder.

Sociologists discuss these kinds of topics with one keyword: taste. If someone enjoys the finer things, they have "good taste." If someone likes trashy TV, they have "bad taste." But who gets to decide which is which? It's a more complicated question

22

than you might think, and it brings us into the murky waters of gender, class, and race. The words *lowbrow*, *middlebrow*, and *highbrow* are eerie synonyms for bad, middling, and good taste. These words find their roots in the racist pseudo-science of phrenology, where people in the 18th and 19th centuries thought you could measure someone's intelligence and worth through the proportions of their heads. Wouldn't you know it, the supposedly smartest head shapes (highbrow) belonged to European men.[5] Does that mean that we've been conditioned to think of "highbrow" art as the best art just because it's made by white guys and not because it's actually good?

This question opens the aesthetic-crisis-of-faith flood-gates. What makes art good? The art itself? The artist's identity? The society that views the art? Academics are still fighting this one out, and I certainly don't have a definitive answer for you (sorry), but here's what we know: There's no clear way to judge art. After all, people respond to the exact same artworks wildly differently over time. For instance, thanks to decades on university syllabi, Jane Austen is now considered one of the most important writers of all time. Her works have been adapted into numerous TV series and films, including *Clueless*. Academics, readers, and viewers alike appreciate her precise narrative voice, romantic stories, and wicked humor. But in her own time, Austen's reception wasn't so warm. Her books didn't make much money, and she was seen as a fashionable writer far more than a literary icon. From the girl next

5  For a famously vile example, see 1839's *Crania Americana* by Samuel George Morton.

door to the Regency's most celebrated author, Austen's rising star shows how differently people see the exact same writing over time.

So, if something's artistic value isn't based on the art itself, but our opinions about the art, what exactly is the difference between the "good" stuff and the "bad"? There are so many theories about this that the field of aesthetics popped up to accommodate them. For now, I'll focus on one major interpretation. For some cultural critics, the difference between "good" and "bad" art is less about plot and more about tone. It's not the story, but the way the story is told.

Carl Wilson explored these questions in a case study on girly art's patron saint Céline Dion. According to Wilson, "bad" art — like Dion's signature anthem "My Heart Will Go On" (1997) — is often hokey or sappy. But, as he notes, sentimental doesn't *need* to mean corny. In another world, sentimentality could mean an honest expression of emotion. We might celebrate how sentimental art provides a "workout to keep emotions toned and ready for use." Think of all the sweet moments in *Clueless* where viewers receive the same exercise: When Cher and Dionne comfort Tai (Brittany Murphy) in the locker room; when Cher and her love interest Josh (Paul Rudd) kiss; when Dionne and her boyfriend Murray (Donald Faison) quietly share lunch. These lovely little sequences encourage us to feel pity, excitement, and affection for the characters onscreen.

Of course, as Wilson notes, "emotions alone are not solutions to issues, but sympathy and compassion are prerequisites to charity and solidarity." In encouraging audiences to feel *something*, to extend concern to a fictional character, soppy art helps us cultivate our ability to empathize. This makes me think of a very old moral tenet found across religions: the necessity of putting yourself in another person's shoes, of treating others as you'd like to be treated. In Western culture, however, sentimentality — especially when it's expressed in rom-coms and pop songs — isn't associated with compassion, but with self-indulgence, exaggeration, and cliché.[6]

What gives? After all, other genres get to be highly emotional and still "cool." Rock 'n' roll ushered in emo music (a genre whose name literally means *emotional*) but rock still has a sheen of righteous anger and detachment from corporate society, even when bands monetize their likenesses to hell and back. (Are you really signalling that you're a counterculture rebel if your Rolling Stones T-shirt was made by an exploited worker in a fast fashion warehouse?[7]) If we think about how emotion is perceived

6 I work in academia where humanities scholars have grown tired of the old thesis that literature is worth reading because it "makes us better people." The resistance comes from the idea that this is a reductive, soppy distillation of an entire, multifaceted field populated by great intellectuals. While I understand the urge to dismiss this idea as a *Care Bears*–esque take on why we should bother reading books, I also think rejecting it outright is silly. Literature *does* provide a way for readers to examine morals and cultivate sympathy. That's an incredible capability and shouldn't be undervalued just because it's not as clinically intellectual as some scholars would like. The fact that the field is so tired of this thesis is itself a sign that we've internalized the idea that brain/criticism/objectivity/rationality is superior to heart/appreciation/subjectivity/emotion. There are clear gendered lines across these arguments — and as usual, the masculine terrain wins out as worthier.

7 We see a version of this play out in *Clueless* when Josh wears T-shirts declaring his charitable affiliations, performatively reads Nietzsche (poolside lmao), and listens to alt-rock by Radiohead. He is signalling his taste (highbrow, philosophical, serious) through the clothing and media he buys. Is this so different from the way Cher signals her own identity (frothy, girly, fashionable) through her own wardrobe and media consumption? Why is one respectable and the other repellent? At the end of the day, everyone performs their identity through the things they buy — but, as always, women get the short end of the stick.

as cringy in Céline Dion songs and big romantic gestures at the ends of rom-coms, but legitimate in music by The Clash, we can see how long-held associations between femininity, irrationality, and frivolity impact the way we rank art. Traditionally, masculine art (like punk music, tragic plays, and hard-boiled noir) isn't considered silly, even though, like schmaltz, it's an exaggerated representation of life. By focusing on rage and melancholy, masculine media becomes the *opposite* of silly. It moves in the opposite direction, deemed respectable, serious, and valuable.

Women have been complaining about this double standard for a long time. In 1929, Virginia Woolf wrote:

> It is the masculine values that prevail. Speaking crudely, football and sport are "important"; the worship of fashion, the buying of clothes "trivial." And these values are inevitably transferred from life to fiction. This is an important book, the critic assumes, because it deals with war. This is an insignificant book because it deals with the feelings of women in a drawing-room.

She's right. And she's been right for far too long. If you swap in *Saving Private Ryan* (1998) for her war book and *Clueless* for her book about women talking, Woolf's point still stands.

The cultural critic Margo Jefferson chalks this up to simple PR. She thinks men have an "aura of presentational licence" that lets them feel comfortable taking up space, sharing their profound thoughts, and insisting that their experiences automatically deserve attention. She's putting words to something we've discussed a lot in the last few decades, such that even writing this paragraph makes me feel like a broken record. Surely by this point, we all know about patriarchy and its discontents. But still, when I try to explain the sheer scale and omnipresence of patriarchy, I inevitably channel that meme where Charlie Kelly from *It's Always Sunny in Philadelphia* (2005–) unveils an unhinged pinboard overviewing a massive conspiracy. I'm still gobsmacked by how this one perspective has tricked us into believing it's the default.

Think about the movies that win big awards like Best Picture at the Oscars. The list is dominated by works directed and written by men (only two women have ever won Best Director) and, unsurprisingly, their subject matter reflects that masculine energy. War films, historical epics, earnest dramas, and biopics (about men, of course) have a significantly higher record of triumph than stereotypically feminine film genres like girlhood comedies, optimistic romances, or movies about female friendship. *Clueless* is regularly considered one of the best rom-coms and teen movies ever made, as well as one of the sharpest comedy scripts ever written. Even so, it received zero nominations from the Oscars, Golden Globes, or Screen Actors Guild.

The reason why is obvious and boring. It's prejudice. We've been conditioned to consider some kinds of art as worthy and others as existing on a spectrum that ranges from harmless entertainment (*Clueless*) to dangerously retrograde fluff (*The Ugly Truth* [2009] which frankly deserves all the bad press it gets). But this overarching bias, like any other, is just a story that's been told enough times that we've accepted it as truth. If art's worth depends on our collective agreement about what counts as significant, then why not change our perspective? If a story no longer works for us, we don't have to co-sign it. Like Gen Z, who — based on delightfully salutary Shrek-centric TikTok videos — seem to have no interest in upholding old-school hierarchies of taste, we millennials can also choose an alternative. For your consideration: apex girly art and the necessary values it cultivates.

For the novelist Rachel Cusk, girly art "by nature, would not seek equivalence in the male world. It would be a writing that sought to express a distinction, not deny it." In other words, when women's literature is different from what we're used to seeing as Serious Important Art, that's a feature, not a bug. The point of girly art is to provide an alternative to the status quo. To understand this alternative, let's spend a little more time thinking about the values endorsed by canonical masculine art and why they may not be the greatest, or at the very least, the only thing worth our consideration.

Let's start with the idea of the hero or the special individual, the man who stands out from the crowd. We see this guy all over the place. He's the lonesome cowboy — Shane riding off into the sunset, Clint Eastwood in grumbling gunslinger mode. He's the brooding antihero — poor little rich boy Bruce Wayne, cut-throat Walter White. He's the anguished artist devoted to his craft to the point of obsession — Andrew, the masochistic musician in *Whiplash* (2014), Mickey Rourke's washed-up athlete in *The Wrestler* (2008).[8] Across variations, one crucial thing remains the same: This man struggles to connect with other people. He's off on his own — walking solo into the sunset, hiding his alter ego from the people he loves, writing poetry into the night. It's not a crime to be introverted,[9] but literature that continually insists that the most interesting, important people are lone wolves makes me suspicious. What's so wrong with finding common ground? With celebrating all that we share? With being part of a supportive community, a sympathetic collective, rather than standing apart? I think we could gain a lot — solidarity, empathy, equity — in tempering one story with the other.

The isolated hero is one step away from a similar masculine character: the tortured genius. Think of artists and philosophers who can see through the dross of daily life to recognize profound truths. These insightful men are often melancholic or mentally ill. Some icons in this school of genius have died by suicide, which is then romanticized and, like a feedback loop, taken as further proof of their brilliance. Consider

---

8 This movie makes me so mad. Rourke plays Randy, a has-been wrestler who's hell-bent on one last victory. Even after he gets into a sweet romance with a nice lady named Pam, he still just has to get back in the ring to prove his commitment to the sport. The climax of the movie: During a match, Randy clocks that he's having a heart attack and instead of getting help, continues wrestling. The movie pitches his death as tragic but noble, an artist's bittersweet apotheosis. I think it's selfish and beyond irritating. Yet another hero narrative where a man does what he wants without considering its impact on the people around him.

9 I dream of being alone.

Kurt Cobain, Vincent van Gogh, Ernest Hemingway, and David Foster Wallace. All this plays into very old associations between seriousness, sadness, and intelligence.

But let's tease these qualities apart for a moment: What's the consequence of assuming that wisdom requires sickness and misery? Considered in this light, the tortured genius is a troubling trope. If brilliant thinkers have to be agonized and alone, then people pursue that one version of intelligence, which means neglecting its opposites: interpersonal and emotional intelligences. You know, the kinds of intellect held by a therapist, social worker, supportive friend. The feminized-and-thus-denigrated[10] "soft skills" and "caring professions" that are crucial to a functional, empathetic society. There's a vicious, snake-eating-its-own-tail style of logic on display here. Because guess what kind of person could help someone in the 'tortured poet' school of genius stay alive and well? Someone who has cultivated the ability to connect with others, to empathize. They would hold the skillsets that could help someone smart but troubled stay alive and well.

In the introduction, I mentioned that the infamous Larry Clark drama film *Kids* came out the same year as *Clueless*. In fact, it was

---

10  And, so often, underpaid. Professions dominated by women (nursing, teaching, secretarial work, childcare, etc.) are considered to be less rigorous and less important simply because they're associated with women — which in turn leads to those jobs being lower paid. A 2016 study at Cornell University proved just how perniciously these ideas affect reality. Researchers found that when women flock to male-dominated fields (likely for the fair pay and recognition they crave and cannot achieve in gendered feminine professions), the pay associated with those fields decreases. Clearly, it's not the work that's the problem — it's who does it. So long as a field is associated with women, that field will be undervalued.

released just nine days after Heckerling's comedy hit the multiplex. This convenient timing provides us with a perfect test case for examining how critics adjudicate competent art about the same subject (an American teenager's daily life) but via wildly different aesthetic, generic, and thematic registers. *Kids* was a risqué critical darling praised for its unvarnished depiction of teens experimenting with drugs, sex, and violence. The end of the film is profoundly nihilistic: 17-year-old Telly (unknowingly HIV positive) persuades a 13-year-old virgin named Darcy to have sex. Meanwhile, Telly's friend Casper rapes Telly's ex Jennie (who was diagnosed with HIV earlier in the film). Ipso facto, all four of these characters — as well as a different 13-year-old girl Telly seduced in the opening scene — either have HIV or have been exposed to the virus by the time the credits roll.

As you can probably tell, *Kids* is not my kind of movie. Critics, though, loved it. The trailer featured awestruck reviews from *Film Comment* ("one of the most important films of the year . . . a stunning artistic achievement"), *New York Magazine* ("honest, relentless, brilliant"), *The New York Times* ("a wake-up call to the world"), *Rolling Stone* ("the real movie event of the summer"), and *The Village Voice* ("a masterpiece!"). Predictably, a film that pitched the teenage experience and the world at large as characterized by brutality, manipulation, and pain wasn't seen as exaggeratedly cruel or a profound failure of imagination but as authentic and poetic. When the same outlets reviewed *Clueless*, their praise was much milder. Perhaps this is why the trailer for *Clueless* didn't feature blurbs from critics — the most promising tidbits are "wicked good fun" (*Rolling Stone*) and "eye-catching and cheery" (*The New York Times*). No one goes out on a limb and insists *Clueless* has artistic merit or social importance. The most it can achieve is charming entertainment. I think this is certainly connected to *Clueless*'s status as a shiny girly movie for shiny girly girls, but also to the film's optimistic emotional register.

It's funny the way fancy art celebrates some emotions but not others. As seen in *Kids*, melancholy and despair are okay. These glum affects signal intelligence and honesty, an accurate response to a brutal world. But other emotions, as we already know thanks to our conversation about sentimentality, are tainted. Expressing positive feelings like joy and hope isn't cool, meaningful, or worth a serious person's time. Instead, there's a clear line running from Clark and Korine's jaded view of the world to critical praise.

But here's the thing about de facto refusing positive emotion: It doesn't let you see the world accurately. Cynicism is an equally stylized way of understanding reality as idealism, just in the opposite direction. Carl Wilson correctly observes that "much modern, critically certified art" exaggeratedly denies what is "acceptable in human existence" (hello, *Kids*!). This misanthropy is just as hyperbolic a way to see things as a fizzy rom-com that tables darkness to insist that everything's perfect. As Wilson writes, ignoring goodness can "breed hopelessness and passivity." Think of the phrase "wallowing in despair" and how it connects a pessimistic outlook with a refusal to do anything, which ironically includes fixing the issues that make us sad in the first place.

Refusing positive emotions like happiness, hope, and relief is, at best, an incomplete way to approach the world and, at worst, dangerously defeatist. When cynicism reaches its logical extreme, we end up with nihilism — a philosophical outlook where nothing matters. For me, that perspective simply will not do. We need an alternative in the face of soul-deadening pessimism. Enter: girly art and its ability to provide viewers with a much-needed spiritual reset.

Life can be overwhelming. Everyone needs to rest at least some of the time. Girly art is here to help you enjoy a deserved reprieve. When I turn on *Clueless* and approach it as a comforting, fluffy movie, it delivers every time (and I've seen this movie like a hundred times). It's funny and smart and charming. The clothes are delightful, the jokes still make me laugh (Cher on remaining a virgin: "You see how picky I am about my shoes and they only go on my feet"), Murray is a treasure, and I coo like a baby when Cher and Josh finally kiss at the end. This movie just injects my veins with sunshine. For 90 blissful minutes, I can escape my troubles and experience simple, sweet Beverly Hills relief.

Sometimes escapism gets a bad rap as willful ignorance to real-world problems. But in moderation, escapism is both necessary and good. Even George Orwell agrees with me — and he's perhaps the world's least likely defender of silly art considering his grim-ass books *1984* (1948) and *Animal Farm* (1945). In essays and reviews, Orwell vigorously defended "light literature" precisely *because* it offers readers much-needed reprieve. In a flawed world, art can provide a balm, can give readers and viewers vicarious frivolity and light-heartedness when they most need comfort. When life feels draining, demanding, and oppressive, girly art has your back. It requires nothing from its audience. Instead, it provides. A sweet rom-com offers viewers pleasure, rest, and laughter. Girly movies let us check out from an imperfect world and experience solace.

Entertainment and diversion don't fully escape capitalism — duh, people make these movies to make money — but when I'm at home watching my old *Clueless* DVD, I do feel free from the grind. I am not optimizing my time by watching Dan Hedaya yell "Get out of my chair!" for the one hundredth time.[11] I am not achieving something productive or frankly achieving anything beyond my own relief. But my own relief, even if it's not immediately productive, is well worth my time and attention. It's a form of self-care, and by this I don't mean the Gwyneth Paltrow method where you buy $500 candles, pound celery water, and insert various rocks into one's pelvis. I'm gesturing towards Audre Lorde's original meaning of self-care as keeping yourself intact so that you have the energy to challenge systems of oppression.

This distinction gets us to different ideas of "good" rest. As much as I understand and support the need to check out of this

---

11 Related, everyone needs to read Jia Tolentino's essay "Always Be Optimizing." It's a brilliant critique of how women are told to optimize every damn second of their time to be hot and make money. Find it in her collection, *Trick Mirror: Reflections on Self-Delusion* (2019).

unpleasant world, I'm also wary of arguments that simplistically defend "guilty pleasures" as a-okay and even transgressive when some of these stories enforce the brutal status quo that makes comfort watches so desirable in the first place.[12] I'm thinking here about the worst that femme genres like rom-coms and soap operas have to offer: one-dimensional glamorizations of selfish partners (*You've Got Mail* [1998]), coercive relationships (*Twilight* [2008]), and women who happily consent to being second-class citizens (*Kate and Leopold* [2001]). If we think about girly art as a mental rest, these movies would score a 4/10. They distract me, yes, but they don't provide deep sleep. For genuinely restorative art, we need to look elsewhere. This pivots us to another way to consider girly art — as generative. Girly art isn't just an opportunity to rest and relax, but to cultivate goodness.

---

12 Tangent warning: Skip this if you don't want to read a meandering screed on lipstick feminism and the wonky, ethical stakes of policing desire. But if you're down, here we go: In Arielle Zibrak's excellent book *Guilty Pleasures* (2021), she defends art that basks in women's suffering, belittlement, and humiliation. For Zibrak, these stories "acknowledge" the "realness" of misogyny, which is valid because "to pretend otherwise would . . . disregard what suffering inside of that reality was really like." That's a fair point — I enjoy period dramas for similar reasons. But I also think that if this is where girly art starts and stops then we're in trouble. If we indulge a person's desire for submission and humiliation dressed up as love, then we tacitly endorse the culture producing that fucked up equivocation in the first place. Zibrak disagrees, arguing that "while there's undoubtedly something wrong with the culture that produces these desires [i.e., for domination, shame], there's absolutely nothing wrong with the person who experiences them, even revels in them." But individual desire isn't something that happens outside of social norms. Our personal desires are so often a symptom of our culture. If you have a problem with one, don't you necessarily have a problem with the other? This all makes me think of a fantastic essay by the scholar Amia Srinivasan on "The Politics of Desire." Her focus is on romantic preferences, but her broader argument is about the standard claim that a woman's "desires" are apolitical and acceptable because feminism means being allowed to want what you want . . . even if what you want causes yourself or others harm. She reasonably asks, "Is there no difference between 'telling people to change their desires' and asking ourselves what we want, why we want it, and what it is we want to want? Must the transformation of desire be a disciplinary project (willfully altering our desires in line with our politics) — or can it be an emancipatory one (setting our desires free from politics)?" I choose B.

35

Girly art has a small scale. Rom-coms and teen movies are about (hot versions of) normal, recognizable people dealing with normal, recognizable problems. Most of the time, the conflict boils down to characters not getting along with their parents, friends, and/or love interests, then learning to communicate more effectively. In other words, characters go through the kinds of everyday struggles that viewers experience. Importantly, though, where real life could end messily, these movies always end happily. People clock their foibles, correct them, and make amends; everyone lives happily ever after. Through accountability and growth, reconciliation and understanding, these characters improve themselves and their little social worlds.

This plotline is so obvious that it almost hides in plain sight. But if you zoom out and summarize the big moves made in foundational girly art of the last 50 years, some shared stances and arguments emerge. Alongside *Clueless*, the plots of teen movies like *10 Things I Hate About You* (1999), *Bring It On* (2000), *Mean Girls* (2004), and *She's the Man* (2006) all move from deception to reconciliation.[13] We watch as young people experiment with lying, cheating, and stealing everything from boyfriends to award-winning cheer routines, only to learn that competition, selfishness, and duplicity are ultimately

---

13 This is a condensed list. So many teen movies have high-concept premises involving performance. *She's All That* (1999) infamously concerns a bet where Freddie Prinze Junior pretends to fall for Rachel Leigh Cook. In *The Princess Diaries* (2001), Mia can't tell her friends she's the Princess of Genovia. *To All the Boys I've Loved Before* (2018) is centered on two teens fake dating. It's almost as if there's a thematic resonance between teenagers play-acting at different identities in high school and movies where characters literally pretend to be people they're not.

unsatisfying. Living life well means rejecting these values and embracing friendship, cooperation, and honesty.

We see something similar with girly bildungsromans such as *Little Women* (1994 and 2019 — both are great), *Practical Magic* (1998), *Uptown Girls* (2003), *13 Going On 30* (2004), *Bridesmaids* (2011), and, yes, *Clueless*, too. These movies all fixate on how women move through moral challenges in their relationships with themselves, their friends, their families, and their workplaces. They take seriously how women navigate the ethical conundrums of daily life. The cure to their ills? Compassion, integrity, and a willingness to be vulnerable. In the movies listed here, immature protagonists of all ages develop by earnestly cultivating these essential qualities.

Romantic comedies like *Moonstruck* (1987), *Clueless* (duh), *My Big Fat Greek Wedding* (2002), *The Big Sick* (2017), and *Plus One* (2019) all consider the complexities of interpersonal communication and romantic love. As a genre, rom-coms hinge on the fact that when people get together and form social bonds, things can get confusing and messy. People have different priorities and perspectives — how can characters balance these disparate needs? How do well-intentioned but imperfect people navigate the give and take of a relationship? These are the kinds of ethical questions people deal with on a daily basis.[14] You can even think of these movies as a glossy, entertaining version of a philosophical symposium. You take people

14 In a way, this makes "escapist fluff" more relevant to most people than allegedly naturalistic dramas. Lookin' at you, *Ordinary People* (1980), *In the Bedroom* (2001), *Life as a House* (2001), *Revolutionary Road* (2008), *The Whale* (2022), etc.

with different histories and beliefs, then put 'em together and see how they handle shared experiences and problems. As anyone who's seen one of these movies knows, things never go smoothly — and that's the point. By watching characters muddle through the messiness of everyday life, viewers can almost run simulations on their own problems.

*Clueless* is a lighthearted teen film, coming-of-age story, and romantic comedy all at once. It combines all these genres *and* their hopeful, moral messages — plus, by adding some satiric bite, it never feels preachy. According to Sarah Pitre, the founder of the Alamo Drafthouse Cinema's Girlie Night series, the movie is the best of all possible worlds: "It's like a guilty pleasure without guilt because it does have substance." Zadie Smith judges mainstream movies with a simple metric: "How much pleasure they give versus how stupid one has to be to receive said pleasure." By this criterion, *Clueless* is a masterpiece. It is a fun, enjoyable movie that in no way requires viewers to turn off their brains in order to appreciate its brilliance.

The literary theorist and philosopher Jacques Rancière once wrote that "an art is emancipated and emancipating when . . . it stops *wanting* to emancipate us." I think this is part of why I tend to find impactful, prescient art in "low" places. Because girly movies were never expected to do more than entertain, they're funnily unburdened by the need to educate or moralize. Ironically, this lets them do just that — educate viewers about morals — in ways that feel effortless instead of turgid and try-hard. George Orwell expresses this well when he writes about fluffy entertainment novels. As he says, this kind of art "attains sincerity partly because they are not inhibited by good taste." When a book or movie's only goal is to provide enjoyment, not to be Significant Important Art for Significant Important People, we can end up with something light and true. Orwell calls this quality "native grace" and says it may have "more survival value than erudition or intellectual power." I see what he means. When I'm troubled, I don't turn to Dostoevsky or Hemingway. I put on my "High Energy Femme Pop" playlist and mainline the nearest rom-com. Girly art helps me get through the hard days. It's a reprieve *and* a pragmatic tool for surviving an imperfect world.

Join me on a brief RPG. It's Friday night and you're having friends over for a movie. What do you watch?

A. *Sophie's Choice* (1982)
B. *Clueless* (1995)
C. *Requiem for a Dream* (2000)
D. *Manchester by the Sea* (2016)

Unless you want to give your guests an anxiety attack, chances are you're going to pick *Clueless*. Girly, feel-good movies are the kinds of movies we watch with other people. This kind of art practices what it preaches: Comedies like *Clueless* help us connect with the people that surround us. They help us stay close to one another.

When *Barbie* came out in the summer of 2023, virtually everyone in the theater was there in a larger group, maybe some combination of mom, sister, friends, and/or partner. When was the last time a Lars von Trier movie compelled you to get the group chat going? Pop culture and girly art take disparate individuals and connect them with their larger societies. They encourage us to participate in public life. And that's step one of building a functional social world, isn't it? The simple act of getting out there and interacting with other people?

Charming romantic comedies and teen films are not inherently inferior to gritty noirs, dramatic Jared Leto vehicles, or anything directed by Darren Aronofsky. They are different in style, not quality. Femme art stylizes our engagement with social problems through specific subjects (relationships, emotions, and daily life) and tones (hope, silliness, and tenderness). Reclaiming supposedly bad art disrupts hierarchies of taste that — surprise, surprise — give top honors to bougie white men. And furthermore, valuing sentiment and optimism isn't just an aesthetic choice. It's a moral one: If we close ourselves to art about connection and joy, we also close ourselves to engagement with qualities like solidarity and empathy — qualities on which democracy itself hinges.[15] Girly art insists that these crucial elements matter.

15 This language is influenced by phrasing in Carl Wilson's fantastic book on Céline Dion, *Let's Talk About Love* (2007).

Girly movies forever. If my manifesto on femme art compelled you to give this unjustly maligned genre a try, here are my top ten recommendations for your next movie night. Note that *Clueless* is omitted as this entire book functions as a recommendation.

*13 Going On 30* (2004): Jenna Rink (Jennifer Garner) and Mark (Mark Ruffalo) are childhood besties who reconnect as adults when Jenna accidentally time travels to the future and realizes her older self has become an asshole. It's like a rom-com crossbred with *A Christmas Carol*, which sounds terrible but is somehow perfect and makes me believe in love. Plus the supporting cast is bonks: Judy Greer, Brie Larson, Sean Rodriguez Marquette, and Andy Serkis all give delightful performances.

*Always Be My Maybe* (2019): Three cheers for Friends to Lovers! My favorite romance trope takes center stage in this warm, silly, sweet rom-com. Sasha (Ali Wong) and Marcus (Randall Park) grow up, grow apart, and at long last reunite when Sasha, now a celebrity chef, returns to San Francisco to open a restaurant. Meanwhile, life hasn't been so kind to Marcus, a talented but unmotivated musician. Workaholic and slacker balance each other out in this very funny, human tale of love won, lost, and won again.

*But I'm a Cheerleader* (1999): Megan (Natasha Lyonne) is sent to a "Pray the Gay Away" conversion camp by her parents. Their plan backfires big time when Megan meets fellow camper and soft butch of her dreams Graham (portrayed by one of my foundational crushes, Clea DuVall). This movie tempers scathing social criticism with tender sweetness. I cry happy tears every time. It also gets bonus points for featuring a pre–*Drag Race* RuPaul and being a tight 90, the correct film length.

*Dick* (1999): Single entendres abound in this tragically unrecognized comic masterpiece. As we'll discuss more in the next chapter, *Dick* is about Betsy and Arlene, two teen girls who inadvertently wangle their way into being Richard Nixon's dog walkers. One of them falls in love with Nixon (brutal) then, thank God, they realize Tricky Dick's a creep and get revenge by becoming Deep Throat and helping Woodward and Bernstein take down the presidency. This movie is the greatest alternate history ever made. Mark Felt who?[16]

*Josie and the Pussycats* (2001): People who don't like *Josie and the Pussycats* hate joy. This hybrid teen comedy/music industry satire/camp classic has a clever script, fantastic pop-punk soundtrack, and an apex 2000s cast: Rachel Leigh Cook, Alan Cumming, Rosario Dawson, Seth Green, Parker Posey, and Tara Reid all turn in charming performances.

16 If you, like me, love to watch disgruntled Dan Hedaya, you are in luck! He plays an utterly beleaguered Nixon in *Dick*.

Bask in the over-the-top outfits and prepare to have "Pretend to Be Nice" stuck in your head for weeks. Also, two *Clueless* alum (Donald Faison and Breckin Meyer) have small roles as members of the boy band DuJour. Their song "Backdoor Lover" (look up the lyrics) opens the film. I love cinema!

*Just Wright* (2010): Applause to this movie for providing one of, like, two love triangles that I do not hate.[17] *Just Wright* focuses on Leslie (Queen Latifah), a self-assured health-care worker who falls for NBA player Scott (Common), even though Scott's in a situationship with Leslie's tactical high-femme cousin Morgan (Paula Patton). When Scott blows out his knee, Leslie becomes his physical therapist and helps him heal — a very subtle metaphor for the restorative powers of true love. This sincere, slow-burn romance is perfect for a mellow night in. Also, everyone say hi to Pam Grier, who plays Queen Latifah's mom.

*Long Shot* (2019): This is mostly here because I'm horny for Seth Rogen. He's completely charming in this movie, which finally lets him play a romantic leading man who isn't awful (see *Knocked Up* [2007]). In *Long Shot*, Rogen is an idealistic, free-spirited reporter who falls for a pragmatic, buttoned-up presidential candidate (Charlize Theron). I love an Opposites Attract story, and this one strikes a

---

17 The other is *The Philadelphia Story*, but a 1940 screwball comedy is maybe a harder sell for movie night.

perfect balance between sweetness and belly laughs. People slept on this movie when it came out in theaters, so if you missed it the first time around, give it a go.

*Magic Mike XXL* (2015): Human potato (that's a compliment, btw) Channing Tatum leads a brotherhood of men on par with the Fellowship of the Ring in this baffling musical comedy. *Magic Mike XXL* sees a ragtag troupe of male strippers go on a road trip, support each other's dreams, and wholly cater to the female gaze. Top toot goes to the scene where Joe Manganiello improvs a routine to the Backstreet Boys' "I Want It That Way" at a gas station.

*Maid in Manhattan* (2002): Imagine if *Cinderella* was also about how we should forgive Richard Nixon for rigging an election.[18] That's *Maid in Manhattan*, baby! In this deranged, stupid, perfect rom-com, Jennifer Lopez plays Marisa, a single mom and hard-working maid at a swanky hotel. Various misunderstandings arise, leading senatorial candidate Christopher (Ralph Fiennes) to believe Marisa is a wealthy guest. They flirt a bunch despite the actors having negative chemistry, Marisa hides the fact that she's (God forbid) working class, and at the end the movie urges viewers/Christopher to equivocate Marisa's white lie with Nixon's corruption and forgive both. This movie is off the wall and utterly joyous to watch with friends.

---

18 I really didn't intend for multiple entries on this list to be about Watergate, but the heart wants what it wants, and my heart wants deeply silly riffs on Watergate.

*To All the Boys I've Loved Before* (2018): Cute. Cute! CUTE. This high school rom-com sees shy, studious Lara Jean (Lana Condor) fake date hot jock Peter (Noah Centineo) to make their crushes/exes jealous.[19] Obvi they end up falling for each other, so plot-wise we're not breaking new ground, but the lead performances are so winning, and Lara Jean's family feels so warm. If you have sisters, this one may be especially up your alley.

---

19 The backstory re: Lara Jean's role in the fake dating thing is absurdly complicated, so the above is a hasty approximation. For the whole deal, watch the movie. It's charming.

# 2

## A Ditz with a Credit Card: Innocence and Ignorance

DIONNE:
*"Rough winds do shake the darling buds of May, but thy eternal summer shall not fade." Phat! Did you write that?*

CHER:
*Duh! It's like, a famous quote.*

DIONNE:
*From where?*

CHER:
*CliffsNotes.*

The ditz is the primordial ooze from which the bimbo, dumb blonde, scatterbrain, space cadet, and stoner crawl. From airheads like London Tipton (the *Suite Life* franchise [2005–2011]) and Phoebe Buffay (*Friends* [1994–2004]) to gentle himbos like Kronk (*The Emperor's New Groove* [2000]) and Josh Chan (*Crazy Ex-Girlfriend* [2015–2019]), pop culture loves a beautiful dum-dum — but why?[20] If we overthink the ultimate underthinker, we learn that ditzes are a gateway into compelling topics like innocence, privilege, and hope.

While there are plenty of variations, the classic ditz has three key characteristics: She is rich, she is conventionally beautiful, and she is untroubled. Expressed as a math formula, the equation for a ditz might read: Rich + Beautiful = No Worries.[21] As such, Cher Horowitz is the platonic ideal of the ditz. She's loaded, thanks to her dad Mel's litigation practice (read: Dan Hedaya yelling at people on the phone). Cher's extravagant house features a double staircase, Greek columns, an immaculate turquoise pool, a sculpture garden, and, most important, a massive, mechanized closet with a virtual program to pre-empt sartorial mismatches. Cher is also stereotypically beautiful, a sentence that feels absurd to even have to write given the evidence that is Alicia Silverstone in 1995. She's just luminous with her halo of blonde hair, glowing skin, and exquisite

---

20 I went down the rabbit hole on ditzes while researching this chapter. For a dangerous drinking game, take a shot whenever I mention a different bonehead. See the following interlude for a data visualization of dummy sub-categories.

21 In the original script for *Clueless*, Heckerling introduced Cher as "beautiful, rich, and damn happy," a direct reference to how Jane Austen describes Emma as "handsome, clever, and rich" in the novel's first sentence.

bone structure. Of course, Cher also fulfills the final element of our ditz equation: Back when Heckerling was pitching *Clueless* as a TV show, the original title was, you guessed it, *No Worries*. Because, yes, while Cher goes through some stuff, for the most part, her problems aren't real problems. Like, she's bad at driving, she gets flushed before a date, and she doesn't get a good grade in debate class. Looking at it all together, I can confidently say: She's fine. Even when things are objectively dire, the movie stays in a light comic register. When Cher gets robbed at gunpoint (!) and has to kneel in a dirty parking lot, she pouts about her designer dress far more than she panics about her life. Her attacker awkwardly stammers "thank you" when he takes her purse and runs away. These characters both know, like we do, that we're in a light-hearted comedy. Even dark moments are played for laughs because nothing truly bad could ever happen in a movie like *Clueless*.

Beyond basic tenets of the girly movie genre, Cher's blissed-out existence is also caused by her head-in-the-clouds perspective. *Clueless* cinematographer Bill Pope emphasized Cher's outlook with multiple close-up shots of the heroine. He used camerawork to "bring the audience close" to Cher and her "amazing point of view, which she takes as obvious, and we take as miraculous." Viewers know that Cher's perspective isn't objective. Instead, she sees the world with such a glass-half-full attitude that bare reality *becomes* fantastic.

As much as Pope admires Cher's sunny outlook, *Clueless* also — true to its title — satirizes the heroine's blinkered view of the world. Amy Heckerling has a lot of fun pointing out

Cher's ignorance with a gentle irony that would make Jane Austen proud. Some of the movie's cleverest jokes occur when Heckerling pinpoints the difference between Cher's idealistic voice-over and the camera's neutral observation. Early in the film, Cher walks out of a party thinking that she's just matched Tai and Elton (Jeremy Sisto). Through voiceover, she proclaims, "I had to give myself snaps for all the good deeds I was doing. It was so great. Love was everywhere!" Meanwhile, the camera shows a drunk guy puking into a pool as horrified swimmers flee. This is a clue that, actually, no, Cher, things aren't going as smoothly as you think — as Cher herself will soon uncover when Elton drives her home and professes his love. Later, Cher goes to a dance with Christian (Justin Walker) and coos, "I mean, look how he ignores every other girl," while her (unbeknownst to her) gay date chats up a cute male bartender.

Scenes like this poke fun at Cher's obliviousness, even as others let us know that she and her friends aren't complete fools. Heckerling makes sure to give equal airtime to the girls' cleverness, like when Cher corrects Josh's pretentious date, Heather, about Shakespeare,[22] when Dionne redefines Cher's virginity as being "hymenally challenged," and when Tai poses a riddle for the ages: "If I'm too good for him, how come I'm not with him?" Even through the satire, you can tell that Heckerling adores her silly, sweet creations. David Denby's

---

22 Heather lectures Josh about how their college professor is "restraining" their "fecund minds" from "wandering through the garden of ideas" (oof) before concluding that, "It's just like Hamlet said, 'To thine own self be true.'" Cher, remembering Mel Gibson in the 1990 adaptation, pipes up that Hamlet "didn't say that. That Polonius guy did." She's right!

*New York Magazine* review puts it well: "Heckerling loves Cher and her friends: Their posing conceals a small gift of poetry."

He's right. There's something profound about these dimwits. For Cher in particular, her poetic appeal lies in her naïveté, a term that means an endearing lack of wisdom, judgment, and experience. To be naïve means that someone lacks the common sense that we take for granted in most functioning adults. This tracks because ditzes like Cher aren't usually seen as adults anyway. Even when they're in their 30s (or even their 60s. See Rose Nylund of *The Golden Girls* [1985–1992]), sweet airheads are more like children. The word "naïve" latches precisely onto this dimension of ditziness. It comes from the Latin for *native* or *natural*; being naive doesn't mean being dull, but returning to a childlike state of wonder and innocence. This is a good-natured outlook that defies the cynicism of adulthood by insisting that change is possible, that kindness can overcome cruelty. A naïve person doesn't know a lot, but in not knowing, they know more than the average person knows. You know?

This is part of why *Clueless*'s production team consistently cast actors with childlike energies. Heckerling described her leading lady, Alicia Silverstone, as "so adorable and sweet and really innocent," while Twink Caplan (who played Miss Geist and acted as associate producer of *Clueless*) recalled the actress's "purity of spirit." Cher's wardrobe cements this theme. Throughout the movie, she's dressed in a whimsical schoolgirl style: empire waistlines, Mary Jane shoes, knee socks. Costume designer Mona May insisted that the "youthful, charming, sweet" outfits did not sexualize the characters, who she saw as fundamentally "childlike." She opted for A-line skirts, cap sleeves, little bows, and headbands because they made the teenage Cher look "like a little girl."[23]

Alicia Silverstone really was perfect for this innocent, childish role, a casting kismet best displayed in the famous debate scene. While arguing that the United States should accept those in need, Cher specifically mentions Haitians, pronouncing the word "hay-dee-ans" when the correct pronunciation is "hay-shens." In a famous piece of *Clueless* lore, this flub was not scripted. Alicia Silverstone genuinely didn't know how to pronounce the word. Heckerling thought the error was perfect considering Cher's ditzy character and let the camera roll.

Even in a culture where everyone's supposed to grow up, immaturity has its perks. Childishness has links to playfulness, enthusiasm, and openness to new experiences. According to the queer theorist Jack Halberstam, juvenile "unknowing" can, funnily enough, lead to a higher-than-average willingness to listen, learn, and reinvent.[24] We see this facet of the ditz

---

23 I have a theory that this was also an overcorrection of Alicia Silverstone's rock 'n' roll image. In 1993–1994, she broke into the mainstream as a bad girl in Aerosmith's music videos for "Cryin'," "Amazing," and "Crazy." Things she does in these videos: skip school, steal a car, get a tattoo and a belly button piercing, beat up a would-be mugger, dress in male drag and eye-fuck Liv Tyler, sky surf, bungee jump, refuse to wear a helmet while riding (and boning on) a motorcycle, etc.

24 Halberstam has a phenomenal essay on how this idea transforms the way we can understand the stoner comedy *Dude, Where's My Car?* (2000). I adore this piece of writing. It's funny and smart and hopeful and it changed the way I thought about scholarship and pop culture. Find it in *The Queer Art of Failure* (2011).

when Cher suddenly opts out of social rules she followed previously. Even though Dionne urges her not to take Tai under her wing ("Cher, she is toe-up. Our stock would plummet"), Cher shrugs her warnings aside to welcome the new kid. Later on, Miss Geist is visibly shocked when Cher, seemingly out of nowhere, volunteers to captain the Pismo Beach Disaster Relief. When Cher previously banished her classmate Travis (Breckin Meyer) to the stoners' "grassy knoll," by the end of the movie she cheers him on at a skateboarding showcase.

From a certain perspective, this could read as flighty. Cher's a teenage girl flip-flopping through different opinions and identities; mean girl one day, do-gooder the next, what's the guarantee she'll actually stick to her new principles? But it's her openness to mixing things up that interests me. Yes, it's dangerous to let yourself be too influenced by others, but it's also dangerous to dig in your heels and close yourself off to change. Through their humility and wide-eyed wonder, ditzes remind us that there's still plenty to learn.[25]


Back in the day, classic authors like Frances Burney, Miguel de Cervantes, John Dryden, and Sarah Fielding set the stage for Cher with a shared character type: the unwitting social critic

---

25 This element of the ditz reminds me of some of Jenny Odell's ideas about identity as characterized by potential and openness. For Odell — an artist and writer fundamentally concerned with one's responsibility to their community — we have to "leave room for the encounters that will change us in ways we can't yet see." The alternative would mean reifying our traits and preferences to such a point that nothing can surprise us. Every day would be the same as the one that came before, which is no way to experience life. Odell describes this kind of set-in-stone outlook as being "basically dead before [our] time." Through their open-mindedness, ditzes are beautifully immune to this existential threat.

whose brilliance lay in their hyperbolic ignorance. These figures lived outside of high society, which let them innocently notice and criticize the unhinged social "norms" that everyone else took for granted. For example, novels by women used this character to reveal the rotten patriarchal foundation of 18th-century life. In Burney's famous novel *Evelina* (1778), the country bumpkin heroine attends a ball and refuses to dance with a suitor she dislikes. This makes complete sense to Evelina and modern readers, even as it causes a scandal in the novel. In the world of the London elite, women were essentially required to accept dance invitations from men, whether they liked them or not. Because Evelina innocently fails to understand this pernicious social norm, she also manages to challenge its outrageous underlying idea: that a man's pleasure matters more than a woman's comfort.

The message behind this sequence (and so many others like it) is to remind readers that it's way too easy to naturalize our social surroundings, to take their cruelty and illogic as inevitable, unchangeable.[26] Ignorant ditzes can use their critical distance from society to reveal that no, that's not how things have to be. If the water we swim in is poisoned, you don't say "oh well" and dive back in. You confront the problem and try to fix it. For these and other ills, sunlight — in the

---

26 The masterpiece *Romy and Michele's High School Reunion* (1997) also picks up on this strain. After trying to get the cruel popular girls to accept them, our heroines finally call a spade a spade. Romy screams, "What the hell is your problem, Christie? Why the hell are you always such a nasty bitch? I mean, okay, so Michele and I did make up some stupid lie! We only did it because we wanted you to treat us like human beings. But you know what I realized? I don't care if you like us, 'cause we don't like you. You're a bad person with an ugly heart and we don't give a flying fuck what you think!"

form of a birdbrain with nothing to lose — may be the best disinfectant.

Cher contributes to this worthy cause in what is perhaps her most famous scene. You know the one. She's walking through the courtyard leading up to her high school, clad in glorious yellow plaid, and soliloquizing about the deficiencies of high school boys. Her voice-over declares, "They're like dogs — you have to clean them and feed them, and they're just like these nervous creatures that jump and slobber all over you." Right on cue, an aforementioned high school boy leaps up and eagerly puts his arm around Cher. In another movie, the heroine might have just let this guy invade her personal space to avoid a confrontation. Frankly, this is probably what I would have done in high school. I am a lifelong conflict avoider and when I find myself in uncomfortable situations, my knee-jerk response is to make sure that other people don't feel awkward, even and especially when I, myself, want to die. In *Clueless*, though, Cher immediately voices her displeasure. She yells, "Ew! Get off of me! Ugh! As if!"[27] and shoves the boy out of frame. You can hear him collide with something, hopefully trash, offscreen. It's an immaculate ten seconds of cinema. Where social codes could easily lead a teenage girl to resign herself to unwanted romantic overtures, *Clueless* draws a line in the sand. If an entitled stranger touches your body, you are well within your rights to yell and push them away.

---

27 Title drop! Note that I include the "ugh." While the quotation is often condensed to just "As if!" I think the "ugh" is crucial: an immediate, angry, non-verbal refusal of this boy's presumptuousness. It makes me think of the way babies and children full throttle, no shame, unequivocally reject things they don't want or like. I strive to own my emotions to this degree.

Ditzes are like mental power bottoms: People underestimate them as idiots, only to realize their error too late. Think of breathy, brilliant Lorelei Lee in *Gentlemen Prefer Blondes* (1953), who knows full well that she "can be smart when it's important, but most men don't like it." Or how Elle Woods, the pert heroine of *Legally Blonde* (2001), wins a murder trial by understanding perm maintenance. One allegedly dumb blonde even outsmarted the House of Un-American Activities Committee during the Red Scare. At an interrogation, the old Hollywood comedienne Judy Holliday confounded questioners by channeling the loopy illogic of her trademark character: the bimbo Billie Dawn in *Born Yesterday* (1950).[28]

My top example of this "Revenge of the Ditzes" trend is the criminally underseen comedy *Dick* (1999), released just four years after *Clueless* and certainly capitalizing on the revitalized interest in clever satires about ditzy teen girls. This movie is a fever dream alternate history of Watergate about vapid high schoolers Arlene (Michelle Williams) and Betsy (Kirsten Dunst) — one character describes their intellect as follows: "I have met yams with more going on upstairs." The teen girls start out as President Richard Nixon's "Secret Youth Advisors" (read: unpaid dog walkers), until a series of hijinks lead them to uncover recordings where Nixon admits to rigging the election. Combined with Nixon's role in the Vietnam War (as Arlene pouts, "War is not healthy

---

28 This is part of a much longer story, but the Red Scare refers to a period in the 1940s and 1950s when the American entertainment industry blacklisted actresses, writers, directors, etc., for allegedly being part of the Communist Party, which often dovetailed with supporting causes, such as civil rights and workers' rights (as Holliday did). When she took the stand and was ordered, as so many were, to identify those involved with the Communist Party, she feigned ignorance to avoid naming names.

for children and other living things") and the fact that he doesn't give his dog, Checkers, enough attention, this is enough for the girls to mastermind his downfall. Arlene and Betsy jointly become Deep Throat, expose Nixon's corruption, and all but force Dick to resign the presidency.[29]

But throughout all this, the girls' main emotion is not anger or sadness. It's something more primal: shock. They're astonished that this kind of corruption is even possible. This ditzy affect makes me think about a quote by the writer G.K. Chesterton. He believed that for people to "resist injustice, something more is necessary than that they should think injustice unpleasant. They must think injustice *absurd*; above all, they must think it startling. They must retain the violence of a virgin astonishment." The girls in *Dick* retain this crucial capacity to be startled, to be astonished, to find corruption not just wrong but absurd, and thus unfit for reality.[30]

For so many people (me included), discovering yet another duplicitous politician leads to shrugs and sighs, a sense that this is the way the world is, and nothing will ever change. Betsy and Arlene don't respond with this cynicism and passivity. Their

---

29 When *Dick* was released, the real Deep Throat hadn't yet revealed his identity. I love imagining that two hippie teenage girls were a prominent "Who was Deep Throat?" theory for six glorious years until 2005, when ex–FBI Associate Director Mark Felt finally owned up to his role in the Watergate scandal.

30 Psychology Detour: In the famous Kübler-Ross model of grief, psychiatrists posit that people move through five stages when they experience profound loss. The first step is denial, a refusal to accept that a trauma has occurred. Over time, the argument goes, the aggrieved person shifts from denial to anger, bargaining, depression, and finally acceptance. The ditz challenges this progression (and maybe the idea that it's progress at all). By remaining stubbornly stuck in denial, the ditz is never forced to find such loss or injustice acceptable. Their refusal to make such pain comprehensible is also a way of refusing the world that made such a loss occur in the first place. It's kind of remarkable. Or maybe my weed gummy is finally kicking in.

purity and ditziness mean they can still be startled and thus can channel their astonishment into tangible political change. After all, these girls literally oust Nixon from the White House. The movie ends with them holding up a sign that says, "You Suck, Dick!" on a rooftop. It's beautiful.

We see a version of this happen with Cher in *Clueless*, especially in the scene where it suddenly gets through to her that the people at Pismo Beach are in peril. It's not just unkind to sit by while they suffer. It's senseless, unreasonable, illogical. This pivot moves us from a shitty moral dilemma (should I pitch in or not?) to an imperative that rings as clear as a bell. When people struggle, the only thing to do is help.

Until now, I've waxed rhapsodic on how ditzes use cluelessness to fight the power, but of course that's not the only way to interpret airheads. Beautiful blockheads have an ugly side, too. It's not a coincidence that so many ditzes look eerily similar; all those thin, white, blonde, upper middle class ditzes are a symptom of a culture obsessed with protecting "pure" and "innocent" white women. We've already encountered — deep breath — Arlene, Betsy, Billie, Cher, Elle, Lorelei, Romy, and Michele. To this list we can add Buffy Summers in *Buffy the Vampire Slayer* (1997–2003), Bianca Stratford in *10 Things I Hate About You* (1999), Melody Valentine in *Josie and the Pussycats* (2001), Paris Hilton on *The Simple Life* (2003–2007), Karen Smith in *Mean Girls* (2004), Shelley Darlingson in *The House Bunny* (2008), Brittany S. Pierce in *Glee* (2009–2015),

Alexis Rose in *Schitt's Creek* (2015–2020), Diane Keaton in any of her scatterbrained roles, Jennifer Coolidge in everything . . . the list goes on and on.

These stereotypical ditzes are cocooned in layers of protection. Their beauty, wealth, and whiteness unite to insulate them from hardship and pain. This adds a sharp note to the typically benign idea of the ditz. Instead of viewing dumb blondes as harmless ingenues, we might consider the thin line between innocence and ignorance. As historian Robin Bernstein reminds us, innocence is not just "an absence of knowledge" but "an active state of repelling knowledge." Seen in this light, sustaining innocence beyond childhood is not straightforwardly good. In this, life imitates art: Remember how I said Alicia Silverstone was perfect for this role because of the Haitians pronunciation debacle? That kind of cluelessness is sweet. But in real life, we've seen that shift from oblivious innocence to dangerous ignorance. There is a world of difference between a 19-year-old Silverstone harmlessly bungling her pronunciation and certain comments the actress has made in the last decade. In a 2014 book on veganism and parenting, a 38-year-old Silverstone wrote that vaccines contain little more than "aluminum and formaldehyde." In 2024, she endorsed Robert F. Kennedy Jr., a notorious anti-vaxxer, for president of the U.S. These stances cannot be seen as innocent ideas put forward by a sweet girl who doesn't know any better, but as dangerous positions held by an adult with a significant platform.

Poet and literary critic Cathy Park Hong writes that "innocence is both a privilege and a cognitive handicap," and that, over time, one inevitably sours into the other. If someone lives in a state of "sheltered unknowingness" for long enough, their innocence distorts into a willful denial of their own privilege. Just think of all the nepo babies who insist that they achieved their success through nothing but hard work. It's easier for people in the upper echelons to downplay their good fortune, because then they don't have to acknowledge the idea that their triumphs weren't earned, but inherited. They conveniently confuse the absence of struggle with the presence of talent or hard work, instead of its real corollary: birthright. From here, it's easy to see how over-the-top innocence tiptoes into outright entitlement, a sense that it would be uncouth for anyone to point out that the playing field wasn't level in the first place. This is the dark side of privilege: Rich, beautiful ditzes happily float through the world precisely because they refuse to consider others' different, more difficult experiences — and the way this inequality directly contributes to their own advantage.[31]

For what it's worth, when Cher falls victim to this kind of ugly self-absorption, it's not played off as a joke. Instead, Heckerling satirizes Cher's insulated worldview, emphasizing its unfortunate limits and omissions. There's one memorable scene where Cher's charm flies the coop entirely. She tells her family's maid Lucy to relay a message to the gardener because Cher "doesn't speak Mexican." Lucy responds angrily,

---

31 Etymology backs me up. *Ditz* is the short form of the German name *Dietz*, which is in turn a variant of *Dietrich*, which comes from the name *Tederich*, which is formed by two elements: *Theud* (people) and *ric* (powerful, rich). Ipso facto, the word *ditz* literally means "rich, powerful person." Privilege was baked into the airhead from the start.

reminding Cher that, uh, she's not Mexican either. After she storms off (fair), Cher looks to Josh for sympathy, but he gives her none: "Lucy's from El Salvador. It's an entirely different country." The film doesn't play this scene as funny or cute. Instead, we witness Cher's ignorance, unvarnished by innocence or charisma. Importantly, Cher is forced to acknowledge her shortcomings, too — and she doesn't like what she sees. The fight with Lucy is one of the last scenes before Cher vows to become a better person.

That said, moments of accountability are few and far between for Cher. For much of the movie, she is unchallenged and remains in her bubble of enabled innocence. In the real world, not everyone has that privilege. A groundbreaking 2017 study confirmed that innocence, like the social privilege to which it corresponds, is far from evenly distributed. While studying trends in how American schools discipline students, three researchers found that authorities are far more likely to see white girls as innocent while Black girls of the exact same age (5–14) are punished more harshly. In judgments, administrators try to justify this discrepancy by stressing that Black girls seem more "mature" than their white peers, alongside other wince-inducing racist beliefs: that Black girls need less nurturing, protection, support, and comfort. According to the scholar Tressie MacMillan Cottom, these racist attitudes do nothing less than erase Black girlhood itself. Meanwhile, by pleading the fifth, white ditzes continue to enjoy the perks of childhood: freedom, forgiveness, and the benefit of the doubt.

When they err, as Cher does, they get an extra chance to do better. Many others aren't so fortunate.

It's not fair. But this unfairness may also be what makes the ditz so enticing in the first place. For as problematic as ditzes are, versions of this character can also offer viewers a reprieve from viewers' real-life worries. The ditz does this by overlapping a particular genre: the Rich White People Fantasy. This term was coined by cultural critic Arielle Zibrak and is pretty self-explanatory but just in case, RWPFs are stories about rich white people who have no real problems. Imagine any Nancy Meyers movie and you get the gist. These films, which invariably feature beautiful homes, luxe lifestyles, loving families, and endless romantic prospects, provide a fantasy of *ease*. Life is just so damn easy for the bankrollers in these movies.

There's a strong intersection between stories about ditzes and stories about rich white people because, well, most ditzes are de facto rich white people anyway. *Clueless* (1995), *10 Things I Hate About You* (1999), *Legally Blonde* (2001), *Zoolander* (2001), *Mean Girls* (2004), and *Barbie* (2023) all pull double duty in both categories.[32] As Zibrak writes, RWPFs — including RWPFs about ditzes — "indulge us by imagining what it would be like to move through the world so effortlessly, to inhabit an experience

32 There's a related subgenre where rich white ditzes suddenly lose their wealth and must hack it with the rest of us plebes. In *The Simple Life* (2003–2007), Paris Hilton experiments with life on the farm. In *Schitt's Creek* (2015–2020), Moira and Alexis Rose go from a mansion to a dilapidated motel. In both examples, though, poverty is either a temporary phase (Hilton obviously got to go home after filming with the working class) or pitched as charmingly pastoral (by losing everything, the Roses gain *so much more*).

so elevated from the experience of everyone else." Movies and TV shows like *Something's Gotta Give* (2003), *Gossip Girl* (2007–2012), and *Emily in Paris* (2020–) are just as outrageous as entries in the Marvel Cinematic Universe. The difference is that, instead of fantasizing about flying around, viewers imagine how life would feel if they were conventionally beautiful, rich, and white. In other words, we get to vicariously experience the superpower that is social power. We can bop around the world without stress or suspicion, bathed in love, attention, and ease.

When I watch *Clueless*, I get to inhabit Cher's light, bright perspective for 90 trouble-free minutes. I enter an escape hatch from my actual problems: precarious employment, clinical depression, the fear of being evicted in a brutal housing crisis — all bog-standard millennial stressors. Watching RWPFs like *Clueless* is perversely soothing because A) it lets me hit "eject" on my real life and experience something easier, and because B) it weirdly lets me off the hook for some of my struggles. RWPFs make it impossible to detangle happy, uncomplicated lives from profound economic and racial privilege. The two are inextricable. You can't have one without the other.

This may be, in a roundabout way, part of why we've seen a surge in ditzes of color in the last two decades. From the 1950s to the 1990s, it was *extremely* rare to see a ditz who wasn't white. There was Ted in *Bill and Ted's Excellent Adventure* (1989) — though, as in so many of his roles, Keanu Reeves's Hawaiian-Chinese heritage was never acknowledged — Hilary Banks in *The Fresh Prince of Bel-Air* (1990–1996), Ed in *Good Burger* (1997), Nisi and Mickey in *B.A.P.S* (1997), and Chastity in *10*

*Things I Hate About You* (1999). That's a very short list compared to all the white airheads I've mentioned throughout this chapter, but it also makes sense. If the stereotypical (and, to be clear, deeply racist) view is that teenagers of color are too mature to be innocent, then ditziness is kind of off-limits. And along with it, so are other attendant qualities we should all be able to experience, cultivate, and enjoy: playfulness, silliness, dreaminess, optimism — and even life itself.

Writing in 2021, the academic Ayanna Thompson connected the belief that innocence is "the sole domain of white people" with "the current social moment" when "unarmed black men, women, and children" are being "killed by police officers in alarmingly frequent rates." For Thompson, these racist beliefs are entwined: as stereotypes empty Black people of innocence, "white innocence" surges in response. Both stories, though, are false: Black people are (obviously) not de facto guilty just as white people are not automatically innocent. These are racial stereotypes, fantastical social narratives lacking a basis in reality. Thus, telling another story — perhaps one of Black joy and freedom — can shift a viewer's beliefs, which can in turn shift public opinion itself, overriding previous, internalized stereotypes with more fulsome representations.

Through ditzy roles, actors of color can challenge racist stereotypes and insist that they, too, are entitled to joyous innocence. Troy Barnes (*Community* [2009–2015]) is a juvenile jock-ditz who thinks an ultimatum is an all-tomato ("as in, you give me the whole tomato, or else"). Hyper-femme chatterbox Kelly Kapoor (*The Office* [2005–2013]) has learned to tune herself out because she talks so much.[33] Sweet Cheyenne Lee (*Superstore* [2015–2021]) thinks that when a tornado hits, the thing to do is "tell someone you trust." Jason Mendoza (*The Good Place* [2016–2020]) constantly drops surreal koans. My favorite is: "I wasn't a failed DJ; I was pre-successful." Lance Arroyo (*The Other Two* [2019–2023]) is a cross between God's own idiot and a hype man. He says "hell yeah" and dabs whenever anyone does anything. Trent Harrison (*Never Have I Ever* [2020–2023]) is Gen Z's Spicoli (*Fast Times at Ridgemont High* [1982]). These characters embody innocence, open-mindedness, and sweetness without the ditz's less admirable baggage: wealth and unrelenting whiteness. They're the natural evolution of this character type; a version of the ditz that I'd like to keep seeing on my TV screen. Long live the (revised) ditz.

If I had to rank Cher Horowitz in the pantheon of pop cultural ditzes, I'd give her an enthusiastic 9/10. My demerit is only because I think Heckerling is a little *too* enamored with her own creation, a little too hesitant to consider her heroine's flaws in much detail or depth. I wonder how the movie would change if its satire of Cher's privilege was more pronounced, if it counterbalanced its affection for her with a little more acid.

But then again, in this situation, the movie wouldn't be *Clueless*. And I do love that the film staunchly insists on its

---

33 Same.

sunshine-and-bubble-gum register. I find it both lovely and moving that *Clueless* manages to be a coming-of-age story without becoming a loss-of-innocence story. The two usually go hand in hand; a protagonist only grows up when they leave their childish naïveté behind and see the world clear-eyed. In *Clueless*, though, people can learn and grow without undergoing a traumatic realization or fully departing from childish wonder. Instead, the narrative halts while Cher's still cooking, so to speak. Her innocence hasn't hardened into the cruel, unquestioning superiority referred to by Hong. She is able to balance good-heartedness with a carefree love of femininity and fun. And importantly, at no point is she forced to reckon with cosmic pain or trauma.

When Marlowe Granados, a writer whose recent work focuses on bimbos and party girls, did press for *Happy Hour* (2021), her delicious picaresque novel about charming naïfs, she often discussed publishers' and readers' resistance to a book that refused to punish glamour girls:

> That's something people criticize my writing for, they're always like, "But they're not suffering enough." . . . People hate that. They always want women to be taught a lesson . . . You don't have to have this story that ends in deep-rooted trauma that you're going to pass on to your children . . . I just think that's not true of the world. To be able to have a negative experience without any bitterness, without feeling any sort of ugliness, is important, I think. That's the world I want to live in, at least.

Granados's staunch resistance of the tried-and-true literary formula where trauma = growth is very much on *Clueless*'s wavelength. Like Heckerling, Granados revels in the lightness pursued by her ditz-adjacent characters. Their charming positivity overcomes scorn; their prioritization of pleasure enriches their lives. Through their unabashed pursuit of enjoyment, *Happy Hour*'s heroines Isa and Gala — like Cher — don't ignore the "real world" so much as they refuse to participate in its bitterness. They ask why this grittier side of existence is privileged as "real" in the first place. Equally legitimate — and certainly real — is the effervescence of living. Ditz characters signify a writer's ethical allegiance to optimism over pessimism, the joy of life over the pain of existence.

In a recent interview, Amy Heckerling grappled with the ditz's pros and cons. While she admitted that ditzes can be "entitled," she nevertheless emphasized Cher's positivity: "There's something so charming . . . [about] people that have that optimism and feel like they can do things, because you know life will beat everybody down eventually." For Heckerling, it's "life-affirming" to "see that quality in people." It's important to remember that Cher genuinely means well, something I find myself taking for granted until I compare her to more conventional queen bee characters. Popular blondes like Heather Chandler (*Heathers* [1988]), Regina George (*Mean Girls* [2004]), and Amber Von Tussle (*Hairspray* [2007]) are evil incarnate. Meanwhile, Cher is still growing and changing, still receptive to others' experiences and ideas. Because of this fundamental trait — alongside Heckerling's occasional critiques of Cher's ignorance — for many *Clueless* viewers, the character explores, more than endorses, entitlement. Overall, Cher is far more endearing than upsetting.

If we wanted to, we could shortchange ditzes as yet another symptom of our profoundly shit world. But Granados and Heckerling — alongside foundational airhead scribes such as Frances Burney and Anita Loos — urge us to see things differently. For these women, hope is more generative than cynicism — and no one's more hopeful than a ditz. And so, while I still have reservations about some of this character's baggage, I'll try to channel some of my favorite gentle-hearted ditzes and conclude things positively. Maybe, sometimes, "airhead" and "open mind" aren't such oppositional words at the end of the day.

While writing chapter two, I kept getting tempted to shoe-horn references to my favorite ditzes in pop culture. To force myself to stay on topic, I developed the following brain-empty-no-thoughts classification system. Someone, please use this to write a book about the cultural history of beautiful dum-dums.

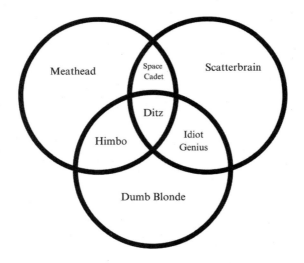

DUMB BLONDE: Because being a Dumb Blonde means holding a silly, feminine state of mind, neither idiocy nor blonde hair are strictly required. Girly girls through and through, Dumb Blondes are part shopaholic, part bimbo, part savvy gold digger, and wholly entertaining. After all, they do have more fun.

*Platonic Ideal:* Lorelei Lee in *Gentlemen Prefer Blondes* (1953).

*Additional Examples:* Rose Nylund in *The Golden Girls* (1985–1992), Hilary Banks in *The Fresh Prince of Bel-Air* (1990–1996), Cher Horowitz and Dionne Davenport in *Clueless* (1995), Buffy Summers in *Buffy the Vampire Slayer* (1997–2004), Nisi and Mickey in *B.A.P.S* (1997), Romy and Michele in *Romy and Michele's High School Reunion* (1997), Betsy and Arlene in *Dick* (1999), Bianca and Chastity in *10 Things I Hate About You* (1999), Miss Rhode Island in *Miss Congeniality* (2000), Karen Smith in *Mean Girls* (2004), Kelly Kapoor in *The Office* (2005–2014), London Tipton in the *Suite Life* franchise (2005–2011), Titus Andromedon in *Unbreakable Kimmy Schmidt* (2015–2019), Alexis Rose in *Schitt's Creek* (2015–2021), Kevin in *Ghostbusters* (2016), Summer in *Girls5Eva* (2021–2024), Karen Shetty in *Mean Girls* (2024), plus Jennifer Coolidge and Dolly Parton in almost anything.

SCATTERBRAIN: Manic energy lives here. The Scatterbrain leads with wacky ideas and off-the-wall intellectualism in place of the Dumb Blonde's sexual attractiveness.

*Platonic Ideal:* Diane Keaton in most movies.

*Additional Examples:* Toni in *Cactus Flower* (1969), Daphne
Moon in *Frasier* (1993–2004), Phoebe Buffay in
*Friends* (1994–2004), Derek Zoolander in *Zoolander*
(2001), Erin Hannon in *The Office* (2005–2014),
Jean-Ralphio and Mona-Lisa Saperstein in *Parks and
Recreation* (2009–2016), Phil from *Modern Family*
(2009-2020), and Barb and Star in *Barb and Star Go
to Vista Del Mar* (2021).

MEATHEAD: Never has a thought sullied the clear mind of this
oblivious jock. Sometimes the Meathead has a violent
streak, sometimes he just likes sports.

*Platonic Ideal:* Drax in the *Guardians of the Galaxy* franchise
(2014–2023).

*Additional Examples:* Reese Wilkerson in *Malcolm in the
Middle* (2000–2007), Van Montgomery on *Reba*
(2001–2007), Dr. Drew in *30 Rock* (2006–2013),
Holland March in *The Nice Guys* (2016), and Shaq
just for general vibes (1972-).

HIMBO: Nice, hunky men untroubled by brainwaves. Beefcake +
Angel = Himbo.

*Platonic Ideal:* George in *George of the Jungle* (1997).

*Additional Examples:* Puddy in *Seinfeld* (1989–1998), Joey
   Tribbiani in *Friends* (1994–2004), Kronk in *The
   Emperor's New Groove* (2000), Fred in *Scooby Doo*
   (2002), Troy Barnes in *Community* (2009–2015),
   Magic Mike in the *Magic Mike* trilogy (2012–2023),
   Josh Chan in *Crazy Ex-Girlfriend* (2015–2019),
   Jason Mendoza in *The Good Place* (2016–2020), and
   Lance Arroyo in *The Other Two* (2019–2023).

SPACE CADET: Tranquil, well-intentioned folks who are mentally out of office for the duration. One key subset of the
   Space Cadet is the Stoner.

*Platonic Ideal:* Bill and Ted in *Bill and Ted's Excellent
   Adventure* (1989).

*Additional Examples:* Spicoli in *Fast Times at Ridgemont
   High* (1982), Harry in *Dumb and Dumber* (1994),
   Ed in *Good Burger* (1997), Kelso in *That '70s Show*
   (1998–2006), Chester and Jesse in *Dude, Where's
   My Car?* (2000), Hansel in *Zoolander* (2001),
   Melody Valentine in *Josie and the Pussycats* (2001),
   Hilary Duff in "So Yesterday" (2003),[34] Kumar
   in *Harold and Kumar Go To White Castle* (2004),
   Cheyenne in *Superstore* (2015–2021), Trent in

---

34 This is the only song, rather than film or TV show, on the list. I include it for the last line of
the bridge which concludes a list of otherwise reasonable hypotheticals ("If you're over me, I'm
already over you / If it's all been done, what is left to do?" etc.) with the profound lyric "If the
light is off, then it isn't on." In the words of the internet, "So true, queen."

*Never Have I Ever* (2020–2023), Philomena Cunk
in *Cunk on Earth* (2022).

IDIOT GENIUS: Academically inclined dum-dums. Idiot Geniuses
blend cleverness and/or surprising book smarts with blind
optimism.

*Platonic Ideal:* Elle Woods in *Legally Blonde* (2001).

*Additional Examples:* Julius in *Twins* (1988), Charlie in
*It's Always Sunny in Philadelphia* (2005–), Brittany S.
Pierce in *Glee* (2009–2015), Dr. Mindy Lahiri in *The
Mindy Project* (2012–2017), Barbie in *Barbie* (2023).

DITZ: All of the above.

# 3

## Way Harsh: Class and Tension

Remember when 1990s and early 2000s teen movies tried to make classic literature sexy for the youths? Shakespearean plays swapped doublets for whale tail and low-rise jeans in *10 Things I Hate About You* (1999; based on *The Taming of the Shrew*) and *O* (2001; based on *Othello*).[35] *Cruel Intentions* (1997) transformed Pierre Choderlos de Laclos's terrible horny aristocrats into terrible horny private school kids (1782, *Les liaisons dangereuses*). Bernard Shaw's *Pygmalion* (1913) integrated hacky sack and Sixpence None the Richer to become

---

35  This is the tip of the iceberg. *She's the Man* (2006) is based on Shakespeare's *Twelfth Night* (1602). *Get Over It* (2001) is based on *A Midsummer Night's Dream* (1605). *My Own Private Idaho* (1991) is based on *Henry V* (1605). (Bonus: there's also a great ECW Pop Classics title by Jen Sookfong Lee on this movie! Read it!) My sister would lose her mind if I didn't mention Baz Luhrmann's *Romeo + Juliet* (1996) and *I* would lose mine if I didn't remind everyone of the *Hamlet* (2000) adaptation where Ethan Hawke delivers the "To be or not to be?" speech while browsing in a Blockbuster. (Couldn't write a more Y2K sentence if I tried.)

*She's All That* (1999). This was cinema's apex — and we owe it all to *Clueless*, the first major 1990s teen movie to draw inspiration from old-school literature.

In Austen's original, Emma Woodhouse is our (anti?) heroine. "Handsome, clever, and rich," Emma lives in a massive estate within the charming village of Highbury. She busies herself by caring for her hypochondriac father, bantering with her brother-in-law, Mr. Knightley, and half-heartedly pursuing "accomplishments." These were like a Regency rewards card: Accumulate enough femme skills — needlepoint, watercolors, pianoforte — and receive a rich husband! But because Emma is beyond loaded, she doesn't actually need to get hitched. Like Cher, she has the luxury of being extremely picky, so until Mr. Right comes along, she devotes herself to "helping" those around her find love. Emma gets a dangerous confidence boost when she pairs her governess (aka nanny/teacher/surrogate mommy) and Highbury's most eligible widower. High on this success, she turns her sights on a naïve, middle-rank schoolgirl named Harriet Smith — a sweet character retooled as Tai Frasier in *Clueless*.[36]

At first, Harriet (like Tai) is flattered to be taken under Emma's wing. The characters become close, but as in *Clueless*, this friendship has a clear power dynamic. Emma is the superior, the tutor educating her pupil-puppet Harriet. Most lessons

36 Only now, during edits of this book, have I realized that Tai's name is formed by three of the letters in Harriet. Previously, I thought it was just a completely random swap.

revolve around navigating life as a young woman, which basically equals finding a husband. Unfortunately for Harriet, Emma is a God-awful teacher. Behold the chaos that follows (and, if it's helpful, see how the aforementioned chaos lines up with *Clueless* by consulting the "Character Concordances in *Clueless* and *Emma*" chart included on page 75).

At the beginning of the novel, Harriet receives a proposal from the well-to-do farmer Robert Martin. This is a solid offer: Harriet genuinely likes Martin and they're a lovely match. Plus, Martin doesn't hold Harriet's illegitimacy against her. (Harriet's mysterious father funds her education but won't acknowledge his daughter — a big no-no in Regency England.) But Emma looks down on Martin and persuades Harriet to decline his offer. *Clueless* reworks this sequence into Tai's meet-cute with Travis Birkenstock in the cafeteria line. They chat about Marvin the Martian, he offers her weed, and it's clear that sparks are flying. And then Cher kiboshes the whole thing: "Loadies generally hang on the grassy knoll over there. Sometimes they come to class and say bonehead things and we all laugh, of course, but no respectable girl actually dates them. You don't want to start off on the wrong foot now, do you?" Message received: Travis, like Robert Martin, will not do.

From this point, the plotlines between *Emma* and *Clueless* line up surprisingly well (though we get a bonus makeover montage in the movie). Emma/Cher matches Harriet/Tai with the social-climbing bachelor Mr. Elton/Elton only to learn that she's completely misunderstood the situation. Mr. Elton wants Emma, not Harriet. When he can't get his ideal girl, he goes for the tacky nouveau riche version: a vile heiress named Augusta in the novel, the try-hard Amber (Elisa Donovan) in the film. Of course, this breaks Harriet's innocent little heart until, like a romantic whack-a-mole, she bounces back. At a country dance/Mighty Mighty Bosstones concert, no one will dance with Harriet/Tai until Emma's brother-in-law and neighbor, mega-rich Mr. Knightley (aka Josh), graciously steps in and saves the day. That's all it takes for Harriet to catch feelings for Mr. Knightley, which in turn leads Emma to belatedly realize that oops *she* loves Mr. Knightley.[37] With the main character's own happiness suddenly at stake, both *Clueless* and *Emma* pivot from an ethically suspect friendship to outright enmity.

---

37 Disclaimer so the Janeites don't come for me: In the original novel, there's also an extended subplot about a character named Frank Churchill (loosely translated into *Clueless*'s Christian). Long story short, Emma and Churchill flirt a bunch, then it turns out he was unavailable the whole time due to a secret engagement with another minor character named Jane Fairfax (no equivalent in *Clueless*). To make things even more complicated (19th! Century! Novel!), Emma thinks that Harriet *also* has a thing for Churchill. The friends never say his name outright when they talk about Harriet's new target, which leads to Emma's horror when she finally figures out that Harriet's secret crush was on Knightley the whole time.

## Character Concordances in *Emma* and *Clueless*

| Character | *Emma* (1815) | *Clueless* (1995) |
| --- | --- | --- |
| Heroine | Emma Woodhouse, 21-year-old heiress in need of belated maturation | Cher Horowitz, problem-free 16-year-old princess |
| Hero | Mr. Knightley, Emma's much older brother-in-law who lives next door | Josh, Cher's ex-stepbrother who still hangs out at her house after their parents' divorce |
| Best Friend | Miss Taylor (awkwardly also Emma's governess) | Dionne Davenport, Cher's ride-or-die BFF |
| Work in Progress | Harriet Smith, déclassé student at the village school | Tai Frasier, grungy new kid at Bronson Alcott |
| Haphazard Suitor Heroine Tries to Set Up With Work in Progress | Mr. Elton, social climbing curate and complete ding-dong | Elton, garden variety egomaniac |
| Haphazard Suitor's Eventual Partner | Augusta, nouveau-riche heiress | Amber, tacky classmate |
| Work in Progress's Eventual Partner | Robert Martin, nice farmer | Travis Birkenstock, nice skater |
| Heroine's Own Haphazard Suitor | Frank Churchill, shiny pretty boy who ends up being secretly engaged to someone else the entire time | Christian Stovitz, well-dressed classmate who Cher does not realize is gay |

Let's go over how book and film each handle the showdown between heiress and underling. In the *Clueless* scene, Tai wears a schoolgirl-inspired tweed set, white knee socks, and a hairband, all reminiscent of Cher's own preppy outfits. Cher, meanwhile, is dressed down — a symbol of the inverted power between these characters. As costume designer Mona May said, Tai "has the power, she's got the plaid; she's on and the other one [Cher] is not." It's a Frankenstein's monster moment: Cher created Tai in her image, and now she doesn't like what she sees. Imitation has gone from flattery to threat as Tai encroaches on Cher's territory in both fashion and romance. After telling Cher that she wants Josh, the frenemies spar:

*CHER:*

*But Tai, do you really think you'd be good with Josh?*
*He's like a school nerd.*

*TAI:*

*What am I, some sort of mentally challenged airhead?*

*CHER:*

*No! Not even. I didn't say that.*

*TAI:*

*What, I'm not good enough for Josh or something?*

*CHER:*

*I just . . . don't think you'd mesh well together.*

You *don't think that* we *mesh well. Why am I even listening
to you to begin with? You're a virgin who can't drive.*

*CHER:*

*That was way harsh, Tai.*

This confrontation has so many layers and, sadly for you,
I will peel through them all.

FIRST LAYER: Tai delivers the rare insult that truly merits
the descriptor *iconic*. The line "You're a virgin who can't drive"
comprises a Great Moment in Cinematic History and a clear
sense of who's the bad guy here: Tai going in for the kill, tar-
geting Cher's most sensitive spots.[38] On the surface, Cher
seems like the victim. All she does is ask if Tai really thinks she
and Josh would be compatible, and Tai flies off the handle with
a vicious burn. Boo hiss Tai; yay hooray Cher.

SECOND LAYER: Tai's insult doesn't come out of nowhere.
Cher may not say it outright ("I didn't say that"), but her comments strongly suggest that the idea of Tai and Josh is absurd.
But . . . why? Josh, who is an undergrad, by the way, goes on
to date Cher, so clearly a girl being in tenth grade isn't a deal
breaker (yikes). So, what's the big difference between Cher and
Tai? According to Cher, it's just an issue of compatibility —
whether Josh and Tai would "mesh well together." But for Tai,
"compatibility" is a smokescreen for talking about her personal

---

38 On the Blu-ray release special features, Brittany Murphy said, "Actually, when I filmed it,
I was a virgin who couldn't drive." Rest in peace, you absolute doll.

worth. When Tai hears Cher say that she and Josh aren't a match, Tai transforms incompatibility into insult: She accuses Cher of implying that Tai isn't smart enough or "good enough for Josh." If we take Tai's side, that's a pretty mean thing for Cher to think about her alleged friend. Boo hiss Cher; justice for Tai.

THIRD LAYER: Whose version of events do we trust? Do we take Cher at her word and believe that she's objectively considering basic compatibility? Or do we agree with Tai and think Cher's implying something crueler about Tai's character? I think we can have it both ways: Tai correctly clocks that Cher is judging her — *but* I also don't think that Cher realizes the depths of what she's saying.

Even in her narration, which usually reveals Cher's inner thoughts, she can't adequately express her problem. When Cher reflects on their fight, she thinks, "This Josh and Tai thing was wigging me more than anything. I mean, what's my problem? Tai's my pal, I don't begrudge her a boyfriend." Cher *herself* doesn't understand why she was such a killjoy, except to fall back on her old excuse: They're just not right for each other. Tai "couldn't make him happy. Josh needs someone with imagination, someone to take care of him, someone to laugh at his jokes — in case he ever makes any."

But Tai *does* have imagination — we see her sketchbook, even if Cher never shows any interest in Tai's hobbies. Viewers also know that Tai can be very caring — she showers her friends with attention and quality time. And in Tai's few interactions with Josh, she's all smiles. The girl laughs at every word out of his mouth; when Cher tells Josh she wants to do something for humanity and Josh replies, "Have you considered sterilization?" the camera cuts to a cackling Tai. So Cher's alleged reasons for Tai and Josh's incompatibility just don't hold up. And yet, Cher's mind is set: Tai and Josh could never work. But Cher and Josh? That's another story. Cher's soliloquy peaks when she admits her real problem with the relationship: She wants Josh.

Let's apply some logic to this problem. To Cher, Tai + Josh = Mismatch. But Cher + Josh = Love. And yet, at this point in the story, Tai is basically a Cher clone, down to the patent leather Mary Janes. So what's the problem here? What's the huge difference between Cher and Tai that makes one Josh's soulmate and the other DOA? The answer revolves around some of the Western world's most taboo topics: money and class.

In the world of *Clueless*, there is an unspoken social and economic hierarchy.[39] Josh and Cher are on one level, and Tai, well, she's beneath them. The final film never comes out and explicitly says "Tai's POOR," but context clues strongly suggest she's nowhere near as privileged as Cher. When Tai arrives at Bronson Alcott, she wears unfashionable, ill-fitting clothes.[40] She has a Bronx accent, which Cher is determined to

39 In the DVD special features of the 2005 *Clueless: "Whatever" Edition*, Amy Heckerling addresses the movie's treatment of class. She admits that class plays a part in the story but that she "didn't want class distinctions to be about money." Instead, she asked herself "who would she [Cher] look down on? And I thought stoners." These are nice intentions that try to get around Austen's treatment of class, but as we've seen, they don't really work out in the final film. The actual movie still strongly aligns stoners (like Tai and Travis) with poverty.

40 Heck, the fact that Tai needs a makeover in the first place is itself a subtle sign of her poverty. The scholar Arielle Zibrak blew my mind when she wrote that makeover scenes in femme movies don't actually want people to look more "physically beautiful." Their true purpose is in erasing someone's lower-class status. What we see as "elevated hotness" is just "elevated power."

eradicate while also "working on" Tai's deficient vocabulary. In a scene where Tai, Cher, and Christian are at the mall, Tai is the only one who doesn't buy anything. In a promotional photoshoot, Tai and Travis are the only characters without cell phones. The best they can do is mime the expensive technology with their index and pinky fingers. The original script is far more blunt about Tai's poverty. Stage directions describe her as a "schlub" with an "unintelligible" accent. When she enters Cher's house, her painful dialogue reads, "Lookit that chandelier, you guys must be rich!"

Tai may dress like Cher towards the end of the movie, but that's not who she really is. Despite her makeover, Tai is still the grungy, henna-haired misfit. Costume designer Mona May says as much when she points out that even when Tai emulates Cher with "the plaid little vest" and "the little skirt," she doesn't come close: Cher's yellow plaid suit is by Jean Paul Gaultier, while Tai's is off the rack. The outfit is still coded as Tai's because it clearly *isn't* "high end." Because of all this, the idea of her and Josh together is a total mismatch, a violation of the natural order. Neither girl says it outright, but this was never a conversation about compatibility *or* personal worth. It was always a conversation about class, about the ways Cher's world unevenly doles out significance, esteem, and love. In guarding Josh from Tai, Cher also guards the one percenters from the unwashed masses.

Heckerling doesn't acknowledge these unsavory elements, but subconsciously the movie knows that Cher's being a bit of a shit. Her delicate talk of who "meshes" well and who doesn't sounds a lot like a speech by another character, one we're meant to find cruel and entitled: Elton. In the car ride home from the Valley party, Elton finds it outrageous that Cher was trying to set him up with Tai:

ELTON:

*Why would I get with Tai?*

CHER:

*Why not?*

ELTON:

*Why not? Why not?!! Don't you even know who my father is?*

CHER:

*You are a snob and a half.*

ELTON:

*Cher, listen to me. Me and Tai, we don't make any sense. Me and you . . . we make sense.*

Who "makes sense" together here is clear. Elton wants a rich girl — someone whose wealth and pedigree match his own. This scene gets at what Cher only implies: that the people who "mesh well together" are two of a kind. No cross-class relationships allowed.

The original novel *Emma* is a lot clearer about these under-currents. In the equivalent scene, we get a peek into Emma's mind and it's a pretty harsh place at this particular moment (which, to be fair, is also one of her lowest points in the novel — no one's at their best when their underling turns on them). Emma viciously scoffs at Harriet's outrageous belief that Mr. Knightley could ever want her: "There would be no need of *compassion* to the girl who believed herself loved by Mr. Knightley." She prays that she'd never set eyes on her: "Oh God! That I had never seen her!" She refers to Harriet as a "burst of threatening evil." But what exactly is the danger here? On one level, it's the idea that Mr. Knightley would be "debased" by marriage to the "inferior" Harriet. Emma worries about how Highbury will turn on Mr. Knightley and subject him to "sneers" and "smirks" if he does end up with Harriet, a lowly girl more suited to marrying a farmer.

But on another level, Emma is terrified and repulsed by the larger threat Harriet poses: a threat to the intricate work of keeping everyone in Highbury in their correct place. The scholar Thomas Keymer gets it right when he writes that Emma is "firmly committed" to "monitoring boundaries" in Highbury. As the queen bee of Highbury, Emma reigns over her little village and uses her power to regulate how each member of the town performs their allotted role. If there are occasional disruptions (the idea of Harriet with Mr. Elton, for instance), they must be a special exception granted by Emma herself. When Harriet takes it upon herself to pursue Mr. Knightley — crucially, without Emma's permission — she messes with the way the village runs.

Early in the novel, we learn that Highbury, like high school, is defined by a rigid social hierarchy. I'll oversimplify the finicky social system of Regency England here, but it usually goes: old money at the top (Emma, Mr. Knightley), the nouveau riche below them (Mr. Elton's new wife, Augusta), then respectable clergymen, military officers, and businesspeople (Mr. Elton himself, Emma's governess). Emma wouldn't associate with anyone below that level (laborers, peasants, the impoverished, etc.).

In Austen's novels, which focus on the top two tiers, all this is expressed delicately with the idea that there are "sets of people."[41] Emma's world includes "the chosen and best" and "the second set." She and Mr. Knightley are the former; Harriet is towards the bottom of the latter. You can imagine the mental gymnastics required to justify this kind of two-tier system without outright admitting that you love inequity: "It's not that the 'second set' are worse — some of my best friends are new money! — but they're . . . different from us. They belong in one part of society, while we belong to another part. You know, the part with pedigree, historic estates, fancy last names. The good part." When Harriet presumes to cross into Emma's realm, she threatens this finely tuned system that requires everyone to accept, as Emma puts it, "the line of life to which [they] ought to belong."

If you're cooling on Emma at this point, fair enough. In a letter, Jane Austen herself admitted that Emma's arrogance

---

41 That language is from Austen's final novel, *Persuasion* (1817), which is also my mom's favorite Austen novel. If you're reading this, hi, Mom!

would tick readers off, writing that she was a "heroine whom no one but myself will much like." Even so, at her best, Emma Woodhouse is a prickly antiheroine and a continually relevant test case in unlikable female characters. Back in the 1980s, some feminist critics tried to reclaim Emma from hordes of naysayers with second-wave ideas. Austen scholar Claudia L. Johnson claimed readers and critics disliked Emma because they were sexists with "a profound discomfort with female authority." For Johnson, Emma isn't an entitled little snot, she's "a woman who possesses and enjoys power, without bothering to demur about it." I think that was empowering in the 1980s but doubles as dangerous inspo for toxic girlbosses today. Just having power isn't de facto good. Feminism doesn't mean everyone gets to act like an asshole. It means dismantling the idea that one person's desires can overpower everyone else's.

For me, this disjunction gets to the problem posed by both *Emma* and *Clueless*: the problem of supposedly benign authority. Both Emma and Cher take it upon themselves to direct their friends and family like pieces on a chessboard rather than living, breathing human beings. Neither do this as some sort of Machiavellian power play; both have, for the most part, good intentions. But their attempts to control people go catastrophically wrong, especially when it comes to Harriet and Tai.

Josh correctly says that Cher treats Tai "like she was your Barbie doll." By the end of *Clueless*, my version of a Tai Barbie would look like Kate McKinnon's Weird Barbie. This girl has not been "played" with; she's been messed up for her owner's entertainment. Poor Tai gets pressured to avoid the one guy she likes of her own volition, then influenced to go after a sentient polo shirt who rebuffs her advances, then shut down when she catches feelings for Josh. Just typing it out exhausts me. I can only imagine how it would feel to actually go through all that — plus deal with teenage hormones.

And yet, through it all, Cher remains pretty likable. Heckerling manages this by changing her source material in a few important ways. Emma is a character who can make you bristle — she's often charming, but she's also an unabashed snob who, as we've seen, thinks social climbers are "evil threats." Heckerling takes this, shall we say, challenging baseline and softens it considerably. At 16, Cher is much younger than Emma's 21. This automatically makes her character more naïve and well-intentioned, less shrewd and antagonistic. When Emma schemes, Cher daydreams. When Emma outright admits that Harriet is too poor for Mr. Knightley, Cher can only say that Tai and Josh wouldn't "mesh" well. At every turn, it's easier to give Cher the benefit of the doubt. But even still, beneath Cher's halo of blonde hair, shades of Emma remain. And because Heckerling refuses to deal with these traces head-on, *Clueless* winds up making some very weird and bad points about the way class affects people's lives.

*Emma* skewers the idea of benign authority by showing how tremendously Emma fucks everything up. The lesson is clear: One narcissist dictating everyone's lives is no good. But in *Clueless*, Cher does pretty much the same thing, and everything turns out hunky dory. In both cases, we have self-absorbed, privileged, oblivious rich girls bopping through life. But where Austen shows, in great detail, all the harm this kind of person can cause, Heckerling struggles to critique Cher. She presents her sympathetically, refusing to vilify her even at her cruelest moments. The critic Jane Hu insists that this pivot makes *Clueless* a better *Emma* adaptation than Autumn de Wilde's excellent 2020 film, *Emma*: "The whole point of *Emma* [the novel] is that Emma keeps missing the point. She's not so much perverse, as de Wilde's more recent film suggests, as she is limited in perspective. As suggested by its title, *Clueless* leans into what makes Emma endearing to Austen."

I think Hu's right about differences between de Wilde and Heckerling, but I disagree with her idea that being "limited in perspective" is de facto "endearing" rather than "perverse." As we learned in the chapter on innocence, being naïve doesn't let you off the hook. Refusing to learn about your surroundings can be just as harmful as outright malice. In fact, I think that's kind of Austen's point: Over-the-top ignorance isn't straightforwardly charming. It also comes with baggage, like Emma's unwavering loyalty to the class system — so different from all Austen's other heroines who achieve the kinds of cross-class romances that Emma expressly forbids.[42] I think Cher's cluelessness does something similar. It's just sidelined to keep Heckerling's movie light and bright.

---

42  In her five other major novels, the heroines are always underdogs who manage to marry wealthy men, often ticking off their new hubby's snobby families. *Emma* is a real departure from this trend.

When you zoom out and think about *Clueless*'s overall message about class, some unsettling arguments emerge. The movie's basic plot supports the idea that Cher is better than Tai, that Cher's emotions and experiences matter more than her friend's. Indeed, Tai is a minor character who sometimes feels more like like a tool or a prop than an actual person. She's important to the story not because she has something specific to offer, but because she helps Cher develop. Tai's wellbeing is sacrificed so that Cher can come of age.

This uneven dynamic reminds me of the larger conversation about "fridging." The term comes from comic book critic Gail Simone, who pointed out a common plotline where one-dimensional women characters (almost always wives and/or daughters) are brutally assaulted or outright killed so that male characters can have profound thoughts and become motivated to do stuff that propels the plot forward. Simone focused on a moment in the *Green Lantern* comics where the hero literally finds his girlfriend's dead body stuffed in a refrigerator, but the conversation has now expanded beyond kitchenware with "fridging" acting as a catch-all term for lazy, sexist writing that uses suffering women as a plot device instead of seeing these characters as mattering in their own right. In recent years, critics have also started pointing out "racial fridging" — when a BIPOC character dies horrifically so a white person can learn a lesson.[43]

---

43 Examples include the movies *The Green Mile* (1999) and *Men* (2022), and the TV shows *Heroes* (2006–2010; see Usutu's entire arc) and *The Falcon and the Winter Soldier* (2021), specifically the episode "Front Line," which kills off Lemar Hoskins (aka the hero Battlestar) so that John Walker (aka the hero U.S. Agent) can feel pain. Related tropes are the "Magical Negro" and the "Sacrificial Negro."

A version of this can happen with class, too. We see it in *Clueless*. Why is Tai around if not to suffer, and through her suffering, to enable Cher's growth? If you rewatch this movie and focus only on Tai, you might be surprised to see that she's miserable for almost the entire runtime. Her pain isn't the movie's focus, but there are suggestions — played for laughs, of course — that this girl is genuinely going through it. After learning Elton doesn't like her back, she sobs in a locker room and slams her head repeatedly on a diner table. The next time we see her, she's getting snubbed at a dance, desperately changing outfits in the hope that someone will notice her. After that, two boys terrify her by dangling her over a railing at the mall. None of this is depicted as true pain.[44] Tai's mishaps are meant to entertain viewers and teach Cher a lesson. Only Cher's emotional troubles are given real consideration.[45]

That's not fair, but you may think it's inevitable. Like, duh, Cher's the main character while Tai has a supporting role. Of course she has less to do than the protagonist. That's just the way narrative structure works. If everyone's the main character, no one's the main character. Someone has to get the short end of the stick and be less important. But it's exactly

---

44 Something similar happens with Travis, the only other poor kid in the movie, when the kids get their report cards back in Mr. Hall's class. Everyone's bummed but only Travis tries to leap out of a window. Again, it's played as a joke; Hall dryly says, "Could all suicide attempts wait until next period?"

45 I think this is part of why Tai only lasts a couple episodes on the TV show continuation, which ran from 1996 to 1999. Tai is included as a lesson, not a character the story's *actually* interested in. Once she fulfills that role, what more is there for her to do?

this — the seeming inevitability of inequality — that I want to trouble.

Stories don't *have* to be structured so lopsidedly. According to the literary scholar Alex Woloch, stories that give special "attention" to one individual character while "flattening" and even "distorting" minor characters rose to prominence in the 18th and 19th centuries as a way of reflecting the time's "actual structures of inequitable distribution," aka the heinous and often dehumanizing class hierarchy of Regency and Victorian England. It may surprise you to know, given how ubiquitous this kind of story is today, that earlier in Britain, other structures competed with stories that focused on a solo protagonist: Miscellanies collected tons of tales with plenty of main characters, ensemble comedies spread the love among half a dozen players, novels told in letters gave each character space to express themselves, and so on. All this is to say, when a story focuses on just one person — and a wealthy person at that — it's not a bad idea to wonder who's left out. If you don't love that Amy Heckerling has mountains to say about Cher's character and the way she develops over the course of the film, only to shrug off Tai as a "malleable" girl who "goes along with things fairly easily," I feel you. It's not a great look. Nothing is neutral, including the way stories unevenly dole out narrative attention.

This focus on Cher's feelings over and above Tai's really colors the way I see the end of *Clueless* when the friends quickly reconcile. At Travis's skateboarding competition, Tai approaches Cher and immediately makes amends:

### TAI:

Look, I have been in agony the last week and I can't even believe that I went off the way I did.

### CHER:

No, I have been going down a shame spiral. I cannot even believe that I was so unsupportive of your feelings for Josh.

### TAI:

No, you are entitled to your own opinion, all right? I'm the tart here. Cher, you've been nothing but super-duper nice to me.

### CHER:

Not even. If it wasn't for me, you wouldn't have even liked that loser, Elton. I'm so sorry, Tai.

### TAI:

Oh, Cher, I'm really sorry. Oh shit, now I'm gonna go ahead and cry.

### CHER:

Let's never fight again, okay?

*TAI:*

*Oh, totally.*

Then girls hug, watch Travis . . . hang ten (? I'm not an athlete), Tai's crush on Travis reignites, sparks fly, yadda yadda yadda, all is well with the world. Clothing provides another clue that things are looking up for Tai: Mona May designed Tai's skater girl outfit in this scene as a balance between her casual pre-makeover style and the clean lines of her post-makeover look. She wears a fitted striped T-shirt, thick metal belt, and loose brown pants. She's not unkempt, as in her opening look, but she's definitely not a Cher clone, as she was in the scene where she wears pink plaid and knee socks. Through costume design, May hoped to communicate that Tai "kind of found herself. She's not trying to be Cher anymore." It all sounds good.

The problem I have with this scene is the script and how it lets Cher off the hook. Heckerling's dialogue almost pitches these two characters as equally wrong, which I find nuts. One righteous burn does not give Cher a retroactive pass to cause Tai 90 minutes of suffering. bell hooks would side with me here. She thinks that "true forgiveness requires that we understand the negative actions of another." This scene happens so fast that I find it hard to believe that Cher and Tai truly understand what led the other to lash out. The so-called reconciliation is treacly, rushed, and unsatisfying. It feels phony in a way that *Clueless* otherwise avoids.

In this scene, I feel strongly that Tai is being made to take what is called the *high road*. She's extending the olive branch, being classy, giving her friend the benefit of the doubt — doing the right thing. But who gets to decide what the "right thing" is in the first place? The cultural critic Tara Thorne has problems with the idea of the high road, specifically charging the concept as a rule "to keep the peace for a certain kind of person. That person is in charge, is unlikely to have earned it honestly, and doesn't want to deal with unrest because it's difficult and inconvenient . . . People in power positions." Hello to you, Cher! In placating her friend and suggesting what each did was remotely on the same level, Tai "keeps the peace" — but at a high cost. Her compliance muzzles her, shuts down an opportunity for Tai to stand up for herself and truly hold her friend to account.

Even so, I understand what this ending is trying to do. The reconciliation scene isn't meant to be hyper-realistic; it's meant to be idealistic. We see an upper-class girl and a lower-class girl overcome their differences and affirm their friendship. Where Cher began the movie surrounded by girls who dressed just like her, she ends it with Tai, who's back in a variation of her original grungy skater girl look. It's like a fable: a teachable story out to prove that rich kids and poor kids can get along after all.[46]

To go back to Austen scholar Thomas Keymer, this is, in its own way, of a piece with the original *Emma*. Keymer argues that Austen's true vision for social wellbeing is "based on harmonious connections between social ranks, whose lives coexist and intertwine in mutually beneficial ways." In the book, Mr. Knightley

---

46 The movie is well aware of its own boppy fairy tale register. On an envelope addressed to Mel, we see that the Horowitzes literally live on Drury Lane — i.e., where the Muffin Man lives in the nursery rhyme.

and Robert Martin fulfill this brief — they manage to be buds even though one lives on a massive estate and the other works on a farm. But in Heckerling's version, that dynamic moves to Cher and Tai. They're the two characters who manage to table their class differences and build a friendship. However, this rose-colored vision of economic solidarity leaves a lot of things unaddressed. What has really changed between Cher and Tai? Don't get me wrong, it's great that Tai can wear clothes she actually likes and date Travis, but on a more basic level, her economic status still means she'll have far fewer opportunities and far more worries than her pal Cher.

This is the tricky thing about Heckerling's view of class. She almost sees it as a value-neutral difference between two people, not a profound inequity. In *Clueless*, the problem isn't that Tai's poor — it's that Cher's mean to her about being poor. But that's not the whole story. In the real world, the problem *is* that Tai's poor. Poverty is stressful and harmful. As we saw during the COVID-19 pandemic, class can mean the difference between life and death. Do you stay home and quarantine while remotely working your white-collar job? Or are you a lower-wage worker who still has to clock into your shift at the grocery store? In Toronto, where I lived in 2020, lower-income earners were hospitalized four times as often as the rest of the population. These people died twice as often as everyone else. So, no, poverty is not a difference that can be solved with open-mindedness and acceptance. It's an injustice that must be remedied with action. In *Clueless*, though, the best we get is a toothless sort of inclusion — an integration that neutralizes any threat once posed by

Tai. Tai can now hang with the rich kids, so long as she accepts her place in Bronson Alcott's pecking order by dating her clear match, the similarly impoverished Travis.[47]

Austen's 1815 novel ends on a grimmer note, but perhaps a truer one. The novel wraps up by reminding readers of the massive social difference between Emma and Harriet and explaining how the two inevitably drift apart:

> Harriet, necessarily drawn away by her engagements with the Martins, was less and less at Hartfield [Emma's estate]; which was not to be regretted. — The intimacy between her and Emma must sink; their friendship must change into a calmer sort of goodwill; and, fortunately, what ought to be, and must be, seemed already beginning, in the most gradual, natural manner.

At every turn, the narrator makes it seem like the cross-class bond between Harriet and Emma was never going to work. The "natural" outcome was always going to be that each girl was shuttled back to her original rank: Emma stays with the gentry while Harriet inevitably returns to her humble roots. This process is "necessary" and "not to be regretted." The mismatched friendship "must sink," "must change." "What ought to be" and

---

47 Like Tai, Travis's poverty is only suggested in the final film. The original script, however, is clearer. It includes a grim scene where he panhandles outside of an ice cream shop. I see why it got cut — it gets too close to the actual experience of poverty to be funny. Like a killjoy, Travis's struggles spoil the happy mood of the film.

"what must be" are one and the same. Reading between the lines, we're being told that the status quo will always reign.

Maybe more unsettling is the idea that the nefarious class system hides in plain sight. It works its power so "gradually" and "naturally" that it's easily mistaken as destiny. No matter what these characters try to do, everyone "must" end up right back where they started. And indeed, at the end of *Emma*, that's exactly what happens. Major characters are paired off in class-appropriate marriages: Well-born Emma gets wealthy Mr. Knightley, low-born Harriet winds up with farmer Martin. But elaborate systems of rank and privilege are not innate or natural. They're constructed. They require a tremendous amount of work (people like Emma who take it upon themselves to make sure that no one steps out of line) and everyone else's compliance (Harriet's eventual acceptance of her own rung in Highbury's social ladder).

Austen's phrasing provides enough dimension and ambiguity to open discussions about these complexities. What is truly inevitable and what's just the status quo? What's been made to seem "natural," and how would things change if we challenged established norms? The ending of *Emma* is thorny, dense, and as mentioned previously, sometimes rotten. It doesn't show us the world as it should be, but the world as it truly is. Given Emma's character, I believe this is the most realistic ending: She would not remain friends with Harriet.[48]

---

48 In the original script for *Clueless*, Josh predicts this will happen to Cher and Tai, too. He says, "As soon as you get bored, you'll forget about her like your pet lizard you forgot to feed."

In insisting that Cher and Tai stay pals, Heckerling breaks with her source material. This is all part of her larger mission: By her own account, Heckerling chose to make a movie that was "so goddamn happy." The original ending of *Emma*, where the heroine and Harriet go their separate ways, would not fulfill this brief, so, fair enough, Heckerling had to make some changes. But by *only* altering the ending without meaningfully retrofitting the torment that Cher puts Tai through, their reconciliation winds up feeling hollow. Even if Tai forgives Cher, I don't know if I do. Tai's trials cast a retroactive pall on the otherwise sunshine-bright world of *Clueless*.

In some interviews, Heckerling almost subconsciously agrees with me on this one. She told one writer that she was "trying to say that *Emma* makes perfect sense now. There's still so much that hasn't changed. Austen was so brilliant, it's timeless." If that's true, why change the ending so significantly? Maybe it's because Austen's "timelessness" is equal parts brilliant and discomforting. After all, the fact that Heckerling can lift a plotline from an 1815 novel and seamlessly transplant it into 1995 reveals how little class has changed in the last two hundred years. We're still dealing with the problems posed by Austen in *Emma*, Heckerling just avoids them to give audiences a feel-good ending. Because of course, in reality, the 1990s didn't solve poverty or class-based inequity. If we choose to remember the decade as a happy-go-lucky time when class difference could be papered over with a hug, we're kidding ourselves. It wasn't like that. It still isn't.

This all goes back to the central tension of *Clueless* as both a satire and a celebration of its core character, Cher Horowitz. Her sweetness and innocence are so endearing; her privilege and ignorance are not. We see this conflict play out when we focus on Tai's tense place in the film. Ostensibly the final act's villain, when we look at Tai more carefully we realize who the true antagonists really are: Cher's elitism and Heckerling's refusal to grapple with her heroine's flaws.

In honor of Tai's sublime dig "You're a virgin who can't drive," I developed the following *Clueless* insult generator. Move through the prompts then fill in the template: You're a (A) (B) (C) who can't (D). Mine is: You're a majorly tardy troll who can't keep it real. It's true.

A) The last digit in your phone number:

| | |
|---|---|
| 0: Big-time | 5: Utterly |
| 1: Furiously | 6: Chronically |
| 2: Majorly | 7: Totally |
| 3: Brutally | 8: Vastly |
| 4: Beyond | 9: Seriously |

B) Your star sign:

| | |
|---|---|
| Aries: Ballistic | Libra: Brain-dead |
| Taurus: Tardy | Scorpio: Sucky |
| Gemini: Superficial | Sagittarius: Cheap |
| Cancer: Wretched | Capricorn: Generic |
| Leo: Miserable | Aquarius: Evil |
| Virgo: Possessive | Pisces: Rigid |

C) The first letter of your name:

A: Monet
B: Snob and a half
C: Hag
D: Fashion victim
E: Lowlife
F: Crybaby
G: Travesty
H: Hag
I: Moron
J: Barney
K: Loser
L: Clone
M: Bonehead

N: Prude
O: Traitor
P: Loadie
Q: Disgrace
R: Farmer
S: Dog
T: Granola-breath
U: Slime
V: Troll
W: Chucklehead
X: Couch Commando
Y: Space cadet
Z: Brown-noser

D) Your favorite character:

Amber: Contribute
Cher: Get in on the heavy clambakes
Christian: Dance
Dionne: Get off the freeway
Josh: Park
Murray: Keep it real
Tai: Hang with us
Travis: Dress

# 4

## Excuse Me, Miss Dionne: Love

As Jewel sings a mopey cover of "All By Myself," Cher meanders around Beverley Hills and hopes that retail will provide therapy. Despite wearing her "most capable outfit," Cher has just failed her driving test, and worse, been called a "virgin who can't drive" by her frenemy, Tai. Through it all, though, Cher's most wigged by Tai's new crush on Josh. "What does she want with Josh, anyway?" our heroine pouts. "He dresses funny, he listens to complaint rock, he's not even cute — in the conventional sense.[49] He's just like this slug that hangs around the house all the time. And he's a hideous dancer, you couldn't take him anywhere." Cher's buggin'. Why does Tai even like Josh in the first place?

---

49 This is objectively incorrect. Josh is Paul Rudd in 1995. He is beautiful.

When Cher reaches a stunning art deco fountain, she admits to herself that Tai's crush isn't so absurd. Okay, okay, she concedes, Josh might be "kind of a Baldwin."[50] But even if he and Tai did get together, they'd be a total mismatch. Then! The fountain behind Cher lights up, water erupts, and like a thunderclap from the gods, Cher has an epiphany: "*I love Josh! I am majorly, totally, butt-crazy in love with Josh.*"

Cher loves Josh, Josh loves Cher, and I love their love.[51] I especially adore the slow, steady way this love develops without either party realizing they're falling for each other. This is a love story that sneaks up on both the characters and the viewer. We almost don't even know it's coming until it actually arrives. By then, the only thing left to do is step back and say, "Oh yeah, these two adore each other." I find such beauty in the ultra-easy, pseudo-subconscious path to love between these two characters because it captures something fundamental about true love: that true love is, in a way, effortless. That true love is freely given. This is *Clueless*'s core argument about love, depicted in all four of the film's romances: Cher and Josh, Dionne and Murray, Tai and Travis, Miss Geist and Mr. Hall (Wallace Shawn).

This vision of love as freely given may seem obvious (duh, if you have to gaslight someone into loving you then you don't really love them) but could not be further from the alleged love stories we so often see in TV and film. Consider

---

50 This reference aged poorly. Swap this with a less-disastrous family of hots: Arquette, Culkin, Cusack, Redgrave, Skarsgård, Wayans, the choice is yours.

51 Mostly. We'll get to the weird ex-stepsiblings part.

the following dynamic: For decades, rom-coms and teen romances have relied on two male character types — the safe and steady boy next door, and the dangerous playboy who learns to love. But it's barely a contest. We know who wins 99% of the time: the bad boy. In the original run of *Sex and the City* (1998–2004), Carrie dumps kind, dim Aidan for vile, dim Mr. Big.[52] In John Hughes's teen dramedy *Pretty in Pink* (1986), Annie rebuffs her loyal BFF, Duckie, for a character so weak-willed he deserves to be named "Blane."[53] In *Reality Bites* (1994), sweet aspiring filmmaker heroine Lelaina Pierce rejects stable, considerate Michael for pretentious theory bro Troy. I'm never not mad about Kathleen Kelly kissing Joe Fox after he burns her dreams to the ground in *You've Got Mail* (1998) — especially when leftie journalist Frank Navasky is *right there*.

Nineties teen TV is all about this trope. Buffy Summers (of vampire slaying fame) preferred not one but two brooding, elderly, undead murderers (one of whom has a creepy situationship with a Buffy sex robot — I wish I was kidding) to bland but reliable Riley Finn. On the classic sitcom *Friends* (1994–2004), Rachel chooses emotionally constipated Ross

---

52 The *Sex and the City* sequel series *And Just Like That . . .* (2021–) provides an interesting spin by killing Big with a Peloton. His untimely death allows Carrie to rekindle her relationship with Aidan — perhaps a sign that our ideas about romance-worthy men are finally changing.

53 The original ending of the movie had Andie and Duckie winding up together. Test audiences hated this, thinking it sent the message that rich kids and poor kids can't get together (Andie and Duckie are both working class while Blane is a rich kid). The studio changed things so that Andie and Blane became endgame. This waters down the movie's correct ideas about working-class solidarity, and the centrality of kindness to a romantic relationship. Blane spends most of the movie avoiding Andie because he's embarrassed that she's poor. Don't date him, Andie.

Gellar over loyal himbo Joey Tribbiani.[54] Aughts and 2010s TV kept this dicey trend alive via the *Gossip Girl* (2007–2012) plotline where Blair Waldorf went for toxic Chuck Bass over decent Prince Louis. On the luminous TV comedy *Jane the Virgin* (2014–2019), our plucky working-class heroine snubs goodhearted Michael Cordero for reformed womanizer Rafael Solano. The recent romance-drama franchise *After* (2019–2023) brings this poisonous dynamic to Gen Z when heroine Tessa rebuffs her gentle boyfriend Noah for a violent alcoholic named Hardin Scott. In *The Summer I Turned Pretty* (2021–), a series of YA novels that have been adapted into a hit TV show, teenage Belly ultimately chooses bad boy Conrad over his nice brother, Jeremiah. And on and on it goes.[55]

Casting directors wisely choose beautiful men to portray these assholes because they know full well that without Hero

---

54 I could write a thesis-length ode to Joey Tribbiani. When he and Rachel get together in season 8, Joey treats her like a damn princess. He communicates openly, helps co-parent her daughter, and straightforwardly adores Rachel. Meanwhile, Ross kept her second-guessing their relationship for 85% of the show's runtime. And she still chooses him? Over her dream career in Paris?? And a beautiful dum-dum who worships the ground she walks on??? No thank you.

55 Two necessary disclaimers. First, please do not willfully misinterpret elements of this chapter to align with that gross Reddit manosphere mindset where "Nice Guys" who bemoan their unrewarded kindness become entitled to the girlfriend of their choice. That's obviously a wretched dynamic and not at all consigned by me or *Clueless*. Second, I'm not saying that TV shows should never use romance stories to explore the dodgier elements of desire, like the perversely pleasurable fall into an overpowering, oh-so-dramatic situationship. That would be a very hypocritical argument for me to make (attraction repulsion is real, and I have the ex-boyfriends to prove it). I know first-hand how turbulent relationships with imperfect people can wind up doubling as an inadvertent bildungsroman that enable young people to try on different identities, experiment with their sexuality, exercise their imaginations, and more. So truly, I'm not out here trying to say that all flawed relationships must be forever banned from television. I more want to examine how rom-coms have equivocated tumultuous affairs with true love. Because when you zoom out and consider rom-coms from the last 30 years, a disconcerting pattern emerges: Bad Boy = Exciting and Sexy. Considerate Stable Person = Boring. Why is this the formula of choice? And what do we lose if we accept it as true?

Fiennes Tiffin's pedigreed cheekbones,[56] or Ethan Hawke's floppy hair, these characters would immediately read as trash. We humans are often a shallow species and, to our collective ill, hot actors help disguise a lifetime supply of red flags.

It's easy to imagine a version of *Clueless* that follows this pattern. In this variant, Cher would reject tree-hugger Josh and pair up with the film's resident rich kid playboy, Elton. Over the film, we'd learn that Elton isn't so bad, that under all the smarm and selfishness he has a heart of gold. Instead of an adaptation of Jane Austen's *Emma*, we'd get a radioactive worst-of-all-worlds retelling of *Pride and Prejudice* (1813). In other words, the story we've all seen a million times before: Girl loves boy. Boy treats girl like trash. Boy eventually learns the error of his ways. Boy and girl live happily ever after — or as "happily" as one can expect, given the quality of man we are settling for.[57]

There are many problems with this formula. One, it's predictable and boring and I hate it. Two, it defies Maya Angelou's always relevant adage: "When people show you who they are, believe them." Three, and most importantly, it poisons viewers'

---

56 His name alone is an accidental parody of upper crust hauteur. In full, it's Hero Beauregard Faulkner Fiennes Tiffin.

57 Theoretically, this could be gender-neutral but I'm queer and I have to say, over many years of watching gay and lesbian rom-coms, I really haven't seen this formula apply to much 2SLGBTQ+ culture (well, except for *Fire Island* [2022], which gets a pass because it's delightful and, like *Pride and Prejudice* [1813], the novel it adapts, it more examines this well-worn romantic plotline than simplistically endorses it). Anyways, as usual I have to ask: Straights, are you okay?

ideas of a good relationship. According to the films and TV shows mentioned before, meaningful, true love is coded as difficult, tense, and rife with conflict. It's good, apparently, to go through years of "will they/won't they" tension, to doubt your partnership's stability, to have to train your boyfriend into treating the people around him with kindness instead of sneering hauteur or allegedly inadvertent shittiness caused by brooding manpain. If you feel crummy most of the time, that doesn't mean you're in an incompatible or outright dysfunctional relationship with a subpar guy — it's a sign that you're experiencing a cinematic sweeping romance.

According to our friend bell hooks, this is precisely the difference between romance and true love. To her, romance is a "project" based on power, manipulation, and coercion. It's like the movies above, where couples continually swap the roles of cat and mouse. They don't experience love, they pursue extravagant, dramatic, and sometimes outright coercive power-plays. It's like a Sisyphean game, a purgatory where neither party is ready to settle down and be together peacefully.

We see this tactical, performative romance when Cher gives Tai horrendous dating advice. After Tai's makeover, Cher cautions her not to date the guy she likes but to leverage her status as a mysterious new girl at Bronson Alcott High School: "If you strike while the iron is hot you can have any guy you want." Of course, it's not really about who Tai wants — we know the guy she really wants is Travis — it's about scheming to nab the most popular boy in school, even if he's a conceited little turd. It's more like a political move than a love story. At a party, Cher repeats this calculation, guiding Tai through strategies to make Elton jealous.[58] Choice tips include "don't say hi first," "make him come to you," "always leave him wanting more," and "Elton's over there, act like Travis is saying something funny." There's no honesty here, no genuine connection between two people, no love. This is as deliberately plotted as a sports play, as hokey and shallow as the dating book Cher tells Tai to read: *Men Are from Mars, Women Are from Venus* (1992). It's a far cry from the reality of giving and receiving true love.

Another sign we're meant to distrust this form of alleged love? Elton endorses it, providing a powerful negative example to Travis's sweet and straightforward communication. In the game of Suck and Blow at the party in the Valley, Heckerling contrasts these male characters. Elton purposely drops the credit card so he can kiss Cher against her will. He games the game to get his way. Travis plays the game honestly, even when it means missing out on what he wants. Breckin Meyer, the actor who so charmingly brought Travis Birkenstock to life, clocked this difference between Tai's key love interests: "If Travis was any good at trying to woo Tai, he would have realized he should have dropped the [credit card]." But we like Travis precisely because this *wouldn't* occur to him. Manipulating a scenario for personal gain isn't attractive. Honesty is much more appealing.

58 She approaches the entire party as a battlefield. One of the movie's endlessly quotable lines is "Let's do a lap before we commit to a location." I recommend employing this strategy at work retreats, family reunions, weddings, etc.

Cher herself falls into this trap when she ineptly tries to woo Christian Stovitz, a fellow student who Cher does not realize is gay. Before their ill-fated date, Cher invites Dionne over so they can do her make-up, choose an outfit, and "design a lighting concept." These girls are stage managing a play, not prepping for a date. Unsurprisingly, Cher's over-the-top fantasy doesn't go well. First, Cher burns a log of cookie dough she plopped in the oven. Then, as the pair watch *Spartacus* (1960; Christian's choice, obvi), Cher awkwardly tries to play footsie with her date. She inches her foot over to Christian and claims, "My feet are cold." Christian responds by sitting up, finding a pillow, patting it on top of her feet, and returning his attention to Tony Curtis. But it's all for the best. Viewers know that this is not the way to go about finding love, even if Christian *was* interested in women.

So, how do we find love? According to bell hooks, true love requires honesty and vulnerability, an openness that lets us "feel in touch with each other's core identity," not a sham performance of who we *think* the other person wants us to be. "Embarking on such a relationship" she writes, "is frightening precisely because we feel there is no place to hide. We are known." In other words, you can't scheme your way into true love. Real love only happens when you open up to another person. From this honest foundation, people can foster relationships that are mutually respectful, supportive, and considerate. For hooks, this healthy bond allows for continual "self-enfoldment." True love helps people become their best, fullest selves.

As pleasant as this is for real life, it presents a problem for Hollywood writers. If the big OTP just got together without any issues, the thinking seems to go, there'd be no story to tell.[59] Apparently, the only option is to use years of conflict to prolong the unions of Bella/Jane/Rachel/Tessa and their respective bad boys. To keep viewers tuning in, executives rely on a steady diet of tension, conflict, and apparent resolution — only to reintroduce tension and repeat the formula ad nauseum.

*Clueless* proves there are more options available by refusing, or cleverly torquing, these tropes. Dionne and Murray, for instance, come across as a dramatic couple who thrive on chaos. Just three minutes into the movie's runtime, they have a public showdown where each accuses the other of cheating. Cher walks away and, via narration, tells viewers she doesn't understand why Dionne bothers going out with a high school boy. Of course, as the movie continues, we learn that Cher (as per usual) hasn't seen the whole picture. Dionne and Murray have a lot of fun together. Their spats are more like a shared hobby or an off-the-books drama exercise than a red flag. In fact, in the original script, Cher catches onto this angle. Her voice-over explains the couple's fights as intentionally "dramatic improv" to "entertain" the school and provide fodder for lunchtime discussion. Consider the following dialogue:

### MURRAY:
*Woman, lend me five dollars.*

---

59 OTP means "One True Pairing." It's millennial internet slang for your favorite romantic couple in media.

DIONNE:

*Murray! I have asked you repeatedly not*
*to call me woman.*

MURRAY:

*Excuse me, Miss Dionne.*

DIONNE:

*Thank you.*

MURRAY:

*Okay but street slang is an increasingly valid form*
*of expression. Most of the feminine pronouns do have*
*mocking but not necessarily a misogynistic undertone.*

After this little speech, Murray sticks out his tongue, hops around, and gives Dionne a goofy, brace-faced grin. As Murray talks, you can see Dionne start smiling. By the time she turns around to hear an astonished Tai say, "Wow. You guys talk like grown-ups," she's beaming.

In other actors' hands, Dionne and Murray's theatrical fights could come across as toxic, but Stacey Dash and Donald Faison imbue them with playfulness and fun. Watching Murray's class clown continually win over regal "Miss Dionne" is adorable. Imagine if casting went with someone else — say, controversial comedian Dave Chappelle (who was in the running for the role of Murray). The vibe would not work. Faison brought a silly dimension to the character, who Heckerling described as "like a puppy" and "a cute little kid." His effervescence makes for a sweet Opposites Attract love story paired with Stacey Dash's dignified performance.

As the movie continues, viewers see how much Dionne and Murray care for each other. In the scene where Dionne accidentally drives on the freeway, Murray guides her to safety. When Cher begins to see each of her friends' strengths, she specifically aligns Dionne and Murray with attentiveness. She narrates, "When they think no one is watching, they are so considerate of each other" as viewers see Dionne and Murray quietly share a sandwich and a kiss.

I'm going to go full-metal-grad-student on this line and point out that there's a meta dimension to Dionne and Murray's tendency to publicly pitch their relationship as dramatic rather than supportive. If movies and TV consistently tell their audiences that real love equals constant fights, then of course two 16-year-olds will act out that vision of love. Maybe this is why Cher makes an otherwise cringey joke about how Dionne and Murray "have seen that Ike and Tina Turner movie way too many times." It's a sign that their performatively "dramatic relationship" is literally shaped by melodramatic media. In the process, being kind to each other becomes something that can only happen "when they think no one is watching." *Clueless* upsets this idea by pitching true love as characterized by compatibility, communication, and consideration, not conflict. Think about how Tai and Travis just *get* each other. They immediately hit it off with their shared grunge aesthetic, love for Marvin the Martian, and appreciation of herbal refreshments. By the end of the film, they share a sweet, intuitive romance — one that, without Cher's meddling, would have gotten off the ground much sooner.

Something similar happens with Miss Geist and Mr. Hall. At first, Cher and Dionne set up their teachers for mercenary motives. But once they're urged to see each other in a new light, their love story moves along effortlessly. Viewers see them share a coffee, kiss by Miss Geist's car, and voilà, at the end of the film, walk down the aisle. Love: It's as easy as one, two, three.

In this movie, love happens so slowly and easily that some characters barely realize it's happening at all. Our central couple, Cher and Josh, fall for each other *that* naturally — which isn't to say that theirs is a soppy, sentimental love story. These two adore each other when they scuffle over the TV remote, argue in the car, and rifle through the fridge. Love grows via endless teasing and verbal sparring. Some of the funniest lines in this very funny movie come from Cher and Josh's rapid-fire, give-as-good-as-you-get banter.

*JOSH:*

*I'm going to a TreePeople meeting. We might get Marky Mark to plant a celebrity tree.*

*CHER:*

*How fabulous, getting Marky Mark to take time from his busy, pants-dropping schedule to plant trees. Josh, why don't you just hire a gardener?*

*JOSH:*

*You know, maybe Marky Mark wants to use his popularity
for a good cause, make a contribution. In case you've never
heard of that, a contribution is the giving of time or funds —*

*CHER:*

*Excuse me, but I have donated many expensive Italian
outfits to Lucy, and as soon as I get my licence, I fully
intend to brake for animals, and I have contributed many
hours to helping two lonely teachers find romance.*

*JOSH:*

*Which I'll bet serves your interests more than theirs.
You know, if I saw you do something that wasn't
90% selfish, I'd die of shock.*

*CHER:*

*Oh, that'd be reason enough for me.*

This perfect dialogue reminds me of some of Heckerling's major influences while making *Clueless*: fast-talking screwballs like *Bringing Up Baby* (1938) and big-hearted romances like *Gigi* (1958). In these mischevious yet sweet movies, true love means exchanging quips *and* acts of kindness. Amid verbal scrimmages, Cher falls for Josh when he gives her a much-needed ride after the party in the Valley, and when he haphazardly jumps around to the Mighty Mighty Bosstones so Cher's friend doesn't feel left out at a dance. Josh falls for Cher when she helps her dad during a complicated legal case, and when she invites Josh over for spring break so he won't be alone on campus. (Josh is avoiding his mom's house because stepfather number four's favorite hobby is criticizing Josh.) Instead of relying on dramatic fights and miscommunication to supply narrative interest, *Clueless* revels in the gradual unfolding of love between two fully realized, well-intentioned individuals. As it turns out, that's enough to intrigue the audience. Steadiness and consideration (plus entertaining digs) trump endless fights and hacky misunderstandings.

This refreshing dynamic is hugely influenced by the characters of our lovebirds, especially our do-gooder male lead. Josh is a rare creature in the world of contemporary rom-coms: an already-good man. Josh leads with kindness and generosity because he cultivates those parts of himself. He's a college freshman who wants to pursue environmental law not, as Mel would say, "to have a miserable, frustrating life" or, as Dionne puts it, because he's going through his "post-adolescent, idealistic phase," but because he's just . . . a good guy. This may sound simple and obvious, but Josh's kindness provides a much-needed reprieve from the Edward Cullens, Joe Foxes, and Christian Grays of the world.

This is part of why everyone's favorite actor Paul Rudd got the role. Twink Caplan, who played Miss Geist and acted as associate producer of *Clueless*, remembered that Rudd was cast because he was "cute and sweet." He seemed softer and kinder than other actors under consideration for the role, including an up-and-coming Ben Affleck. Indeed, there's more than a little overlap between Paul Rudd and Josh. Rudd actually owned the Amnesty International T-shirt that Josh wears in the movie. Both actor and character were "crunchy" (Rudd's word) or, less derisively, interested in making the world a better place.

Josh's gentle disposition extends to how he approaches romance, specifically in two scenes involving the grand staircase in the Horowitz home. First, Paul Rudd could give a masterclass in the look of love. When Cher walks down the staircase in a white dress, Josh is in awe. Just gobsmacked by how lovely she looks. This is his fountain epiphany, and even without narration, it's clear what he's thinking: He loves Cher. He is majorly, totally, butt-crazy in love with Cher.

Second, let's consider Cher and Josh's first kiss. A first kiss is everything. It sets the tone for the romance that follows by testing the chemistry between our leads (Is it a good kiss? Is this thing going to get off the ground?) and, more interestingly, by establishing power dynamics (Who takes the lead and goes in for the kiss? Who follows suit?). It's important that Cher and Josh's first kiss pitch their forthcoming relationship as remarkably equal (and yes, it's a good kiss, too). When they sit on top of the twin staircase, the camera frames them symmetrically — each actor takes up the same amount of cinematic space. The overall effect is of a mirror: Even Cher and Josh's body language reflects each other. Both characters sit in the same position (scooted up legs, bent knees, slightly arched backs) and look directly at one other.[60]

After some awkward hemming and hawing from Josh, Cher softly admits that she cares for him. It's the most vulnerable she's been in the entire movie. When Josh claims that he goes to Cher's house all the time because Mel's "the only one that cares about me," Cher responds with a quiet, "that's not true." No bravado, no witty retort. After asking "Are you saying . . . you care for me?" Josh goes in for the kill. And by "the kill," I mean a tentative peck. Josh pulls away and gives Cher a look as if to say "What do you think? Is this okay?" She smiles, and they kiss again, for real this time.[61]

When Paul Rudd's agent saw the movie, he specifically took issue with this scene. Thinking such a gentle kiss would tarnish his client's chances at heartthrob roles, he cried, "Oh, you didn't kiss her right. You should have grabbed her!" Incorrect, sir! Josh is appealing precisely because he wouldn't pull that kind of macho nonsense. Viewers have already seen a boy repeatedly grab and kiss Cher in this movie — that boy is Elton, and we hate him. Josh is our leading man because he is Elton's antithesis: humble to his conceited, gentle to his aggressive, kind to his cruel. Of course his kissing style would follow suit. This kiss is magical because it proves what I've

---

60 Cute detail: In the scene where Cher and Dionne see Miss Geist and Mr. Hall sharing a thermos of coffee, they coo over their body language: "Legs crossed towards each other, that's an unequivocal sex invite." The actors are posed almost identically to Cher and Josh in the big kiss scene! Cher is finally living out the sweet love story she created for others.

61 Then, if you are me rewatching this scene for the hundredth time on YouTube, a jump scare Joyce Carol Oates suddenly starts declaring things about fiction. It's an ad for her Master Class — I'm too cheap to get YouTube Premium.

been saying for this whole chapter: Gentleness is itself desirable. Also, we are all on Team Consent, yes? Paul Rudd proves that checking in is (and has always been) both good and hot.

The movie's very last frames show another kiss between Cher and Josh, and this one really sets me a-titter. After Cher catches the bouquet at Miss Geist and Mr. Hall's wedding, she and Josh share an all-time great Hollywood embrace. Heckerling frames this shot so that we're at eye-level with Cher and Josh who, again, equally share cinematic space. Josh gently touches Cher's face and hair. Cher slips some tongue. (Get it.) They seamlessly pivot to many tiny kisses on cheeks, necks, ears. Cher does an adorable giddy little hop as they hug. We fade to black. It's a perfectly happy (and subtly horny!) ending for this sweet couple.

I love Josh and Cher for many reasons, including their adherence to two of my favorite rom-com tropes. Blessed trope one is Enemies to Lovers. (I love when people fall for each other through mutual insults.) Blessed trope two is Friends to Lovers. God, I am such a sucker for this one. To me, it just makes so much more *sense* to fall for a friend, someone you already know is kind and worth your time, than to go all-in on a stranger. Pop culture backs me up hard on this one: Jenna and Matt in *13 Going on 30* (2004), Sasha and Marcus in *Always Be My Maybe* (2019), Jess and Nick in *New Girl* (2011–2018), and David and Patrick in *Schitt's Creek* (2015–2020) are all primo examples of Friends to Lovers. I'll tune into this trope until I die.

But of course, I'm kind of hedging here because as you probably know, Cher and Josh aren't just Enemies to Lovers and/or Friends to Lovers. No, they are also the worst of all romance tropes: the cursèd Family to Lovers.[62] The fact that Josh and Cher are ex-stepsiblings has cast a justifiable pall on this otherwise sweet couple. So, let's address the ick. When Josh and Cher were kids, Josh's mom, Gail, and Cher's widowed dad, Mel, got married. According to Cher, they weren't together for very long ("You were hardly even married to his mother!") and when the real plot of *Clueless* kicks into gear, it's been five years since Mel and Gail split. Because Cher is 15-going-on-16 during the movie, this means that Mel and Gail ended their marriage when she was 10 or 11. Through this creaky backstory, you can almost hear Amy Heckerling urging audiences to be okay with this scenario. "They lived together for like a second when they were kids!" she seems to say. "It's not like they grew up together! I swear this isn't *Flowers in the Attic!*"[63] Even so, it's a little weird. "Siblings or Dating?" should be a joke on the internet, not a legitimate question.

When asked about this, shall we say, unique backstory for her central couple, Heckerling remembered executives

---

62 While researching this chapter, I learned that the following people also married their cousins: Johann Sebastian Bach, Charles Darwin, Albert Einstein, Saddam Hussein, Jesse James, Jerry Lee Lewis, Edgar Allan Poe, Franklin D. Roosevelt, Greta Scacchi, H.G. Wells, and Queens Elizabeth II and Victoria. For a terrible bonus game, guess which two men on the list above married literal 13-year-old girls.

63 When we were preteens, my sister was down bad for this book. To the best of my recollection, it's about Aryan-looking siblings who are locked in an attic by their mean stepmother, then the isolation and teenage hormones basically lead the brother and the sister to make out? (I'm not looking it up, my cookies are bad enough already.) Anyway, there are like 20 books in the series by V.C. Andrews so clearly Shannon was not alone in her thirst.

at Fox flagging a similar concern: "They thought that was incestuous. Like: 'What if the Brady Bunch got involved with each other?' I didn't watch *The Brady Bunch* so I couldn't really argue. The thing is, my grandparents were stepbrother and stepsister."

Hm? What's that now?

According to Amy Heckerling, this really wasn't so unusual in a particular time and place. Her grandparents lived in the Pale of Settlement, an area of western Russia bordering on countries including Lithuania, Poland, and Ukraine. The "settlement" was, in actuality, an enforced Jewish ghetto that existed until 1917. Due to widespread antisemitism, Jewish people were forbidden from living beyond the area's borders. Generations of Heckerling's family grew up here, including her great-grandparents and grandparents. Within this area, it was normal for extended family to step in when a mother became a widow. As Heckerling put it, "If your brother died and he had a wife and children, you would marry the woman and take care of the kids." That sounds fair enough, and indeed, her family followed this practice. With all this in mind, join me as I decode some family math.[64]

Heckerling's grandmother's father lost his wife around the same time as her grandfather's mother lost her husband. They both had teenage children, so they decided to get married and share the load rather than going it alone. This meant

---

64  Hot Tip (?): "Family math" is a handy euphemism for figuring out if you're related to a romantic prospect. My partner, who is from a smaller community on Cape Breton Island and has something like 120+ first cousins, had to do a lot of family math to get through high school without committing a crime.

the families blended, and suddenly a group of young people (importantly, as per Heckerling, "totally not blood-related" young people) started living under the same roof. Heckerling's grandparents were two of these young folks. They met as stepsiblings and eventually got married. Her grandmother spoke of her grandfather as her "protector," and they were together until death did them part. With this background in mind, it's easier to understand Heckerling's rationale for pairing Cher and Josh. To her, it's not an automatic no-go.

The awkwardness of this couple also gets to Heckerling's Regency source material. In novels by Jane Austen, you'll often encounter gross-to-modern-eyes pairings. In *Mansfield Park*, for instance, the heroine, Fanny, marries her cousin, Edmund. In *Sense and Sensibility*, 50-something Colonel Brandon weds the teenage Marianne Dashwood when he *should* be marrying Marianne's mom. In *Emma*, we get a questionable mix of these two unions. As we know from chapter three, Cher is based on Austen's self-obsessed heiress Emma Woodhouse while Josh is based on her much older neighbor Mr. Knightley. Knightley and Emma are lifelong friends related through marriage — Emma's sister marries Mr. Knightley's brother, making them siblings-in-law. At the end of the novel, they get married (turn that family tree into a twisted pile of roots!) and yes, it is a little gross to modern eyes.

But in both *Emma* and *Clueless*, I'm much less skeezed out by the baffling step/in-law complexities than I am by the age differences at play. Like, sure, you want to fall for your sister's husband's brother — whatever. You're both consenting, non-biologically related adults. Do what you want. But in the novel, Emma is 21 while Mr. Knightley is middle-aged. He was a full-grown man when she was a baby. He even brings up the fact that he held her infant body right before he proposes! Thank Christ, *Clueless* isn't nearly this extreme, but Cher *is* in tenth grade while Josh is a freshman in college. This means she's 15/16 while he's 18/19. Those are a crucial three years of maturing. If modern-day me knew a 15-year-old dating a guy in university, I'd tell her to run.

If I could tweak one thing about this movie's central romance, I'd make Josh younger. All the hobbies and quali-ties that differentiate him from Cher — reading Nietzsche, planting trees, getting into activism — can just as easily be held by someone in high school as someone in university. In the scene where Cher disparages the way high school boys dress, one actor wears a *Peace Protest* T-shirt. Another wears a shirt that pithily demands racial reparations, reading *Damn right I have an attitude. My parents worked 400 years without a pay-check. Reparations now.* This is left-leaning Josh-coded apparel, if I ever saw any, and it's worn by boys Cher's own age. As such, exaggerating the age gap between Cher and Josh, to me, doesn't serve much of a narrative or character-based purpose. It's just a gross detail that the movie could easily do without. When an uncreative remake of *Clueless* inevitably hits, my Christmas wish is that the writers will at least pivot Josh to a student at a neighboring high school (maybe one of those artsy ones where everyone paints and organizes protests?) rather than the local university.[65]

But overall, I really do love the romance in *Clueless*, imperfect though it may be. It's so cathartic to see an already-good man celebrated as the real love interest instead of sidelined as the nice-and-thus-boring guy. It's so sweet to see two people fall in love without conflict and miscommunication, to see compatibility and kindness championed as interesting in their own right. It's so satisfying to watch a Radiohead-listening, grunge-wearing, activist boy recognize the beauty of naïveté and femininity, qualities too often dismissed as frivolous. It's so nice to watch two people make each other better: to see Josh's tree-hugger qualities rub off on Cher when she pursues the Pismo Beach Disaster Relief campaign, to see Cher's girly pep challenge Josh's "deep and intellectual" pursuits, like reading Nietzsche and growing a painful goatee. May we all be so lucky to experience this kind of true love.

Throughout her work, TV critic and Pulitzer Prize winner Emily Nussbaum argues that the media we consume shapes our feelings and desires. In other words, witnessing romance, even if it's filtered through a TV screen, can't help but shape

---

65  Unexpectedly, Amy Heckerling seems to have agreed with me. In an episode she wrote and directed for the first season of the *Clueless* TV show, she cheekily cast Paul Rudd as an anti-Josh named Sonny (get it, Sonny and Cher?). He's a college guy who plays guitar, rides a motorcycle, and dates Cher without realizing she's a sophomore. He ends their relationship when he figures out that she's just 16 while he's almost 21, saying, "I think you should date someone your own age." Indeed! Why we couldn't figure this out before the *Clueless* script was finalized I will never understand.

our own ideas of love. As we turn on our screens, we might take a moment to consider just what we're inviting into our hearts and minds. Will we accept the tension and conflict that stand in for romance in media like *After*, *Jane the Virgin*, *Twilight*, and so many other TV shows and films? Or will we choose to validate and ennoble steady, straightforward love stories centered on already-good men, rather than works-in-progress?

By cosigning *Clueless*'s vision of love, we insist that we deserve considerate, communicative partners. This deceptively light rom-com urges viewers to value the self-enfoldment of true love, not to settle for the power plays of a hollow romance. In doing so, we don't just ennoble the considerate male leads sidelined by so many romances — we offer ourselves a kinder, truer understanding of how to give and receive love.

## INTERLUDE: ROM-COM HEROINES WHO CHOSE THE WRONG GUY

There is no light without darkness, no happiness without grief, no swoon-inducing *Clueless* love stories without evil rom-coms where heroines choose terrible men as better options wait in the wings. In the spirit of using garbage to recognize beauty, join me on a journey through five rom-coms where the heroine chooses the wrong guy and ruins what could have been a nice story.

### 1. *Roman Holiday* (1953)

> Premise: Joe Bradley (Gregory Peck) is a roving reporter in need of a scoop. After a zany series of mishaps, he encounters tourist Anya (Audrey Hepburn), leading the duo to strike up a tender flirtation and enjoy one perfect day in Rome. There's just one problem: Anya is really Princess Ann, a royal on the run from her oppressive keepers. What's more, Joe knows full well that Anya's only pretending to be a commoner. Will these crazy kids ever come clean and make it work?

> Who She Chooses: Monarchy.

> Who She Loses: Joe Bradley.

**Why She's Wrong:** If *The Crown* (2016–2023) has taught us anything, it is that mid-20th century royal families do not give two cents about their young'uns' personal happiness. Furthermore, this movie was secretly cowritten by noted leftie Dalton Trumbo, feeding fuel to my fire that *Roman Holiday* shows us what *not* to do instead of celebrating Anya's noble sacrifice. Resist the powers that be! Gregory Peck and freedom > royal duty, especially when said duty is coded as the gong show British royal family.

## 2. *Boomerang* (1992)

**Premise:** The rare rom-com centered on a man, this Eddie Murphy vehicle sees the comedian play suave businessman and rampant womanizer Marcus. Marcus is used to calling the shots, until he dates Jacqueline (Robin Givens) and gets a taste of his own medicine. Will Marcus change his ways in time to start a genuine relationship with kind and artistic Angela (Halle Berry)?

**Who She Chooses** Obviously, Angela and Marcus end up together.

**Who She Loses:** Well, Angela misses out on forming a power couple with Jacqueline.

Why She's Wrong: *Boomerang* almost tells a satisfying "leopard changes his spots" story only to rush through its third act and screw the pooch. Marcus ricochets between Jacqueline and Angela, cheats on everyone, and seemingly learns no lessons before sneaking into Angela's workplace and begging her to give him another chance. As a sign that even the film's writers couldn't figure out why she'd agree, Angela says, "Give me one reason why I should take you back." Marcus, like *Boomerang*'s viewers, is silent. This happens two minutes before they suddenly kiss and the movie ends.

## 3. *Reality Bites* (1994)

Premise: Lelaina (Winona Ryder) is an aspiring filmmaker who must choose between capitalism and "high art" in both her career and her romantic life. Will she go for Michael (Ben Stiller wearing a suit) and shill for a paycheck? Or will she follow her heart and hook up with Troy (Ethan Hawke with peak hair)?

Who She Chooses: Troy.

Who She Loses: Michael.

Why She's Wrong: Troy uses the fact that he is Ethan Hawke in 1994 to convince Lelaina (and scores of viewers) that a pretentious art bro is better than a stable, considerate guy with a job. We're meant to see Michael as a corporate sell-out, but sue me for liking the man who wants to help Lelaina make enough money to pay rent while also pursuing her aspirations to direct a documentary.

### 4. *You've Got Mail* (1998)

**Premise:** After investing in a lifetime supply of emotional barriers, Kathleen Kelly (Meg Ryan) lets her guard down and begins a flirtatious AOL correspondence with a mystery man. But just when her personal life ramps up, her professional life tanks. Headed by smug businessman Joe Fox, a massive chain bookstore opens near Kathleen's independent children's book shop. The Barnes and Noble clone endangers her livelihood and confirms Manhattan's soulless gentrification.

**Who She Chooses:** AOL Mystery Man Who Is Obviously Joe Fox.

**Who She Loses:** Frank Navasky (played by Greg Kinnear at his most charming).

**Why She's Wrong:** I have never understood the fuss over this "love" story. The soundtrack is fine, I will grant you that, but what is romantic about capitalism crushing Meg Ryan's small business? Man, there is a world of difference between Michael in *Reality Bites* and the monster that is Joe Fox in *You've Got Mail*. This is a movie for people who'd swoon as their loaded boyfriend burned their dreams to the ground and said, "It was just business, it wasn't personal" (a real line from this movie's climax).

## 5. *Something's Gotta Give* (2003)

Premise: Erica Barry (a luminous Diane Keaton) is a successful playwright whose daughter brings home a much-older man named Harry Sanborn (Jack Nicholson). When Harry, after a lifetime of womanizing and boozing it up, finally has a heart attack, he stays at Erica's beach house to recover with the help of local Hot Doctor Julian Mercer (Keanu Reeves). After Erica's daughter dumps Harry, he slowly learns to — *gasp* — consider dating a woman his own age. In the meantime, Harry faces stiff competition from Julian, who's into Erica as well. With her pick of the litter, Erica reconnects with her fun-loving, sensuous side.

Who She Chooses: Harry.

Who She Loses: Julian.

**Why She's Wrong:** Keanu Reeves plays a beautiful doctor who just wants to take Diane Keaton on nice vacations and pay her compliments. Julian asks Erica out by writing his number on a prescription pad, implying that A) a date with him is just what the doctor ordered and B) his employment is gainful and based on both hospitality and intellect. He also specifies that dinner will be at seven, solidifying that Julian knows the correct time to pitch a date for a woman over 60. Jack Nicholson spends most of his time realizing that he is a Bad Man and sweating.

# 5

## Not to Your Face: Friendship and Silence

*Clueless* is a perfect example of how the 1990s thought about race in that it staunchly refuses to think about race at all. You may have noticed that Cher's last name is Hamilton on her report card only to become Horowitz during attendance, pivoting her from a WASP to a Jewish-American princess. This change was an off-the-cuff ad lib by Wallace Shawn during the scene where Mr. Hall takes attendance. Why did Heckerling keep this alteration in *Clueless*? The better question may be: Why wouldn't she? Cher's ethnic background makes no material difference to the plot because in the world of the film, it's a moot point — an afterthought, optional, unimportant to her character. *Clueless*, as a true product of its time, doesn't see race.

We have prominent Black characters like Dionne Davenport and Murray Duvall, but the idea of racial difference itself is tabled: There's a quick note that Dionne is "African American" in the script, the reparations T-shirt I mentioned in the last chapter, and one poster in Cher's high school that says "End Discrimination." (Eagle-eyed viewers can peep it in the background of the scene where Christian walks into class for the first time.) Beyond these fleeting moments, race is never meaningfully addressed in the film. Paul Rudd even tried to audition for Murray because he thought the character was a white poser — and to be fair to Rudd, the script made no comment on Murray's race. The real-life basis of Mr. Hall — seen briefly as the principal who introduces Tai during PE class — is a Black man nevertheless played by the white actor Wallace Shawn. No one in the film — from Amber to Elton, Summer to Miss Geist, Josh to Mel's rude legal student — even acknowledges that these characters have cultural or racial identities in the first place. The thinking seems to go something like this: If no one sees race, no one can be racist. We've got a classic case of color-blind diversity.

This approach has limitations that, believe me, we will explore in detail. But it's also important to contextualize *Clueless* and recognize that it was a fairly progressive movie in its own time. The film hosted an unusually diverse cast, with scholar Lesley Speed highlighting Cher and Dionne's interracial best friendship and the explicitly gay character Christian Stovitz. For many viewers, this is a net good. By not making a big deal of Dionne's race or Christian's sexuality, their characters also avoided stereotypes and provided marginalized viewers with rare, not actively awful, representation in a major Hollywood movie.

Dr. Wendy Osefo, Johns Hopkins Professor of Education and Real Housewife of Potomac (seriously, she's both), said that *Clueless* was the movie that made her feel like she had a place in popular culture. This was largely due to Dionne, who Osefo sees as "not just the stock best friend" or "appendage to the lead." Instead, Dionne's affluence and romantic life provided Osefo with a clearer understanding of her own aspirations (capitalistic though they may seem). The comedian Ziwe fawned over Dionne, praising her as a "Black woman who was absolutely glamorous on screen." Dionne was "the baddest thing walking, the coolest girl in high school." An ultra-girly girl, Ziwe admitted that "a lot of my personality is based on that fictional character," and specifically shouted out Stacey Dash's underrated comedic chops: "Everyone talks about Brittany Murphy's line readings and Alicia Silverstone's performance, but no one really talks about how fucking incredible Stacey Dash is." Credit where credit is due, Dash has impeccable comic timing. I love her smiley delivery of, "Cher's main thrill in life is a makeover, okay? It gives her a sense of control in a world full of chaos."

The journalist and cultural critic Ta-Nehisi Coates agrees with Osefo and Ziwe in saying that Heckerling takes a character that could "in a lot of teen movies" be "the subject of derision" or a "side character" and instead gives her "all sorts of complexity." To all these viewers, Dionne is dignified, self-assured, caring, beautiful, and no-nonsense all at once. She gets to be a specific person, not a token or a trope. The same can be said of Murray. He's articulate, silly, self-serious, and so, so funny.

My favorite Murray scene is when he shaves his head at the Valley party because he's "keeping it real" and then panics when Dionne threatens to call his mother. He's doing what so many kids do in high school: trying on a grittier identity and walking it back the second your parents enter the equation.

Likewise, Christian avoids some brutal stereotypes of gay men in the 1990s. Murray summarizes them in the scene on the freeway: "He's a disco-dancing, Oscar Wilde–reading, Streisand-ticket-holding friend of Dorothy, know what I'm saying?" But the actual character Christian does none of these things. He's not just a shopping buddy or one of the girls. Christian has a bafflingly unique personality and aesthetic: A '90s teen who thinks the death of Sammy Davis Jr. left a spot in the Rat Pack, he loves Old Hollywood, experimental sculpture, and "getting the 411 on the local clambakes." Christian is a specific, weird person, not a lazy joke or corny object lesson in tolerance.

In the scene where Cher tries to seduce him, Heckerling doesn't play the misunderstanding for big laughs. Instead, it's one of the film's most grounded moments: a quiet, awkward interaction between two teenagers wading through the hormone soup of adolescence. GLAAD even sent Heckerling a letter praising her depiction of Christian as a gay friend who does more than shop. They specifically liked the character's big hero moment when he rescues Tai from two knobs at the mall.

When *Clueless* came out, gay men formed a major fan base. In an interview with *Vogue* celebrating the film's 20th anniversary, Silverstone said, "That has always been my favorite aspect of the film. Particularly what it means to gay boys." In 2021, Silverstone recreated the scene where Cher tries to seduce Christian on TikTok and cast her own "real-life Christian": best friend and fashion designer Christian Siriano. "We love each other so much, and I'm sure some of that stems from him really admiring *Clueless* and what Cher meant to him and all of his friends growing up," she explained.

Comedians and writers Matt Rogers, Louis Virtel, and Bowen Yang (of *Saturday Night Live* fame) agreed on multiple *Las Culturistas* podcast episodes between 2021 and 2023.[66] Even when *Clueless* isn't the specific subject of a show, the movie keeps popping up as a favorite, specifically for its humor, costumes, and diva main character. Funnily enough, Christian isn't a huge part of *Clueless*'s appeal to gay men (though Virtel does shout out Cher's line that "he thinks everything should be beautiful and interesting" as an appreciation for the gay aesthete). Instead, it's Cher and Dionne who resonate most. Addressing how the film sees Christian, Matt Rogers sets the bar quite a bit lower: "For a movie in 1995, it's not homophobic which is huge."

We can understand the lukewarm reception of Christian by thinking about how another cultural critic interprets the movie's treatment of race. Ta-Nehisi Coates credits *Clueless*'s progressive view of race to how Heckerling lets Black charac-ters be "accepted as themselves. As their own, human selves."

---

66 Matt Rogers and Bowen Yang are both regularly on TV, so you may know them a bit more than Virtel. As an introduction, please note that Virtel went viral in 2015 for unleashing a ferocious finger snap after winning a Daily Double on *Jeopardy!* The moment quickly became part of gay internet lore.

I think that's a nice, generous thought, and I don't want to underestimate why it appeals to Coates. He's implying self-determination beyond identity markers, the idea that (of course) people are more than just their race, or their gender, or their sexuality. To obsessively define someone by one aspect of their identity would be reductive. So, fair enough, Coates prefers to think of Dionne and Murray as "human" characters more so than the film's potentially tokenized Black characters.

But at the same time, I wonder if this is a glass-half-full view of how *Clueless* handles race and, extending on Coates here, queer sexuality. After all, it's only a small jump from Coates's claim that the characters are first and foremost "human" (i.e., just like anyone else) to the idea that race itself doesn't matter. It's like your uncle who insists that we're all one race, the human race. Or like Stacey Dash, the actress who played Dionne and infamously worked as a Fox News pundit from 2014 to 2015. During that time, she heartily endorsed *Clueless*'s color-blind treatment of race, saying, "That's Amy's genius, that race doesn't matter."[67] The film does something similar with Christian: The fact that he is gay is explicit but anything beyond that — any consideration of how Christian's queerness impacts his life — is out of bounds.

In an ideal world, race and queerness would not matter because racism and homophobia would not exist. But we do

---

67 In 2021, Stacey Dash said that she regrets a bunch of horrendous statements made during her tenure on Fox. She doesn't specify beyond that, but I'm hoping disavowed quotations include her declaration that the wage gap could be fixed if women "worked harder," the many times she suggested that if Black people "stop[ped] complaining about white people" racism would go away, and her insistence that trans people pose a danger to her children and thus should pee in bushes instead of restrooms. I genuinely hope she's changing her tune and doing better.

not live in that ideal world, so applying this attitude to the here-and-now is at best flawed and at worst actively harmful to actual anti-bigotry efforts. As culture shifts from a watery mandate for tolerance to a more sensitive attention to the complexities of how racism in particular manifests in the world, we're learning that a one-size-fits-all approach to inclusion isn't working out.

Even the word "tolerance" suggests something dodgy is afoot. I'm a white person and I think we really told on ourselves when this became the buzzword for race relations in the 1980s and 1990s. Tolerance literally means putting up with something or someone that you find appalling.[68] The base problem isn't dealt with here — racist ideas are repressed, not corrected. When someone claims not to see race, or other markers of oppression like queerness, they can also fail to see ongoing racism or understand bigger problems like systemic discrimination. Years of sociological studies confirm it: Ignoring race doesn't make racism go away.[69]

Funnily enough, *Clueless* ends up teaching viewers this exact lesson. Despite purporting to take place in a world where

68 Not coincidentally, "tolerance" is a term used a couple times in *Clueless*, again signalling the film's allegiance with the reigning racial politics of the day, flawed though they may be. After Travis's out-of-left-field speech about generational differences via the Rolling Stones versus the Nine Inch Nails, Mr. Hall politely responds with, "Tolerance is always a good lesson, even when it comes out of nowhere."

69 See several studies by Harvard Business School professor Michael I. Norton and his research team in the 2010s. Cultural critic Mychal Denzel Smith's work provides a handy bird's-eye view of the broader issues at play with color-blind attitudes to race.

race plays no part, *Clueless* features a fair few discriminatory tropes and patterns. Think about the cast. In the original script, Heckerling specifies the race of only five characters. Scene directions introduce Dionne as "a stunning, African American girl." Josh tells Cher that Lucy is from El Salvador. The Persian student Paroudasm Banafshein makes fun of Mr. Hall in Farsi. From context clues, we know that the Horowitz family's gardener is Mexican, and that Christian is white (the original script featured a line where Cher says, "Usually white guys are terrible dancers, but Christian is killer"). The rest of the film's 20 plus other parts are unspecific about race, which means that, hey, anyone could play them, right? This is a color-blind movie, so in theory everyone has the same shot at these roles. But in practice — and you'll know this if you've seen the movie — the *vast* majority of these speaking parts go to white actors. Again — ignoring race doesn't automatically solve racism. Its true function is to avoid a challenging subject.

While Dionne isn't the Sassy Black Friend, she *is* relegated to a supporting role — something we see in so many movies that try to be inclusive.[70] Jonathan Lethem calls this ubiquitous trope the *Tubbs Placement*, referencing the show *Miami Vice* (1984–1989), where Philip Michael Thomas played Ricardo Tubbs as second lead to Don Johnson's protagonist, James Crockett.

70 While researching this chapter, I read a few articles that pitched Cher and Dionne as co-leads. Jen Chaney, who collected *Clueless*'s oral history in several interviews with the cast and crew, described their friendship as one between "strong, supportive equals." I'm puzzled by this characterization because, objectively, it's just not accurate — but maybe it's useful. Retconning *Clueless* as a two-hander lets people avoid grappling with the movie's weird treatment of race.

Getting the Tubbs Placement means being "just a tad behind the white guy in significance and charisma." Aisha Harris, host of the NPR podcast *Pop Culture Happy Hour*, strongly criticizes this trope and specifically cites Dionne as a primary example of The Black Friend. For Harris, this uneven dynamic between allegedly equal friends ends up relegating Black characters "to the sidelines." It's a "gesture of feigned inclusivity and the bare minimum in terms of character development."

The racialized sidekick can be seen, but only in relation to the inevitably white main character. Think about how we only glimpse Dionne's life when she enters Cher's, rather than the other way around. This leaves viewers like Harris with a pile of unanswered questions: "Who were these characters' families, I wondered? What were their aspirations? Did they have crushes? How did they feel about being the Black friend? Did they really like the boy they were coupled up with, or did the uninspired casting just call for the one Black girl in the story to be linked up with the one Black guy?[71] Did they have *any* friends of color outside of this core group of white people?" Because Cher never asks Dionne these questions, viewers never get answers. Dionne's visibility depends on Cher's interest. And Cher's perspective, as we already know, is neither accurate nor neutral.

Cher's view of race relations isn't as color-blind as the film would like to suggest.[72] There's a telling sequence early

---

71 For the record, I don't think this is the whole story in *Clueless*. Murray and Dionne are a super sweet couple.

72 To be clear, any white person claiming to not see race is low-key admitting to some shady shit. To be "neutral" in a system of oppression is to tacitly side with the status quo.

in the film when Cher gets a C from Mr. Hall and feels "impotent and out of control." She needs "to find sanctuary in a place where I could gather my thoughts and regain my strength." As orchestral music swells, we transition to the Beverley Center, Cher's favorite mall. Dicey fact (can't really say "fun" given the context): The music in the scene is "Tara's Theme" from *Gone with the Wind* (1939), a movie that infamously grieves the Confederate loss of the American Civil War. You know, the war where the Confederates wanted to keep bondage going while the Union fought to abolish slavery? *Gone with the Wind* sees both these sides and decides to pitch the Confederates as a noble and tragically defeated cause. The music "Tara's Theme" plays whenever the heroine, Scarlett O'Hara, yearns for home, the cotton plantation that enslaved over a hundred people. It's not a great look — not now, not in 1995, and not in 1939 upon its original release. Activists have raised the alarm about *Gone with the Wind*'s wildly racist revisionist history since it hit the screen. And yet, there it is in *Clueless*.

In linking this particular music with Cher's own safe space, Heckerling says more than she realizes. Like Scarlett O'Hara, Cher's innocence, happiness, and "sanctuary" are enmeshed in a larger system of brutal racial oppression, as we learned in chapter two. And like Scarlett, Cher has her own troubling Black sidekick. Aisha Harris incisively traces the legacy of the sidekick Black friend to earlier media fixated on white masters and Black servants — one infamous example being Scarlett O'Hara and Ruth, more commonly known as

140

Mammy.[73] For Harris, culture has moved from professional servitude to emotional servitude. Dionne is not Cher's literal underling but her status as a supporting character nonetheless repeats troubling dynamics. She's secondary to the white lead, her job in the story is to facilitate that character's development. But because *Clueless* doesn't see all the problems with this messy *Gone with the Wind* homage, it can't amend the scene. That's the trouble with color-blindness — if you don't recognize racism's ongoing history, you can wind up perpetuating the problem.[74]

What's funny is that this refusal to clock social problems isn't maintained evenly throughout *Clueless*. If the idea is that refusing to engage with difficult issues will, like magic, make them disappear, then why is the film so gung ho to challenge some stereotypes but not others? Fans have long claimed *Clueless* as a proto-feminist chick flick for its clever skewering of gender stereotypes. Written and directed by a woman (rare now, wildly rare in 1995), the movie depicts an unapologetically feminine teenage girl as ambitious, clever, and funny.

---

73 This specific characterization of both Black women and slavery is so flawed that the term "Mammy" has become shorthand for a bevy of racist stereotypes including the happy slave and the brusque, sexless, maternal caregiver.

74 An oft-used escape hatch for these critiques is to say that the author meant to do all this, that this kind of scene isn't an endorsement of unequal race relations but a super subtle criticism. I don't think this is the case with *Clueless* because, while the movie often makes fun of Cher's perspective, it has *nothing* to say about race at this point or any other. Plus, in decades of interviews, Heckerling has never addressed this music as a layered critique of Cher's oblivious view of race. This is, more simply, a flawed joke that accidentally reveals a ton about the film's feeble take on racial oppression.

Her characterization refuses the well-worn idea that someone like Cher is automatically an idiot and challenges the broader connection between femininity and frivolity itself.

Several scenes acknowledge and critique sexism. When boys grope Cher, she shoves them away and lambastes how they feel entitled to her body. When Heather underestimates Cher's intellect based on her appearance, she swiftly puts her in her place. But *Clueless*'s satire is most vicious when Heckerling depicts Cher's obsessive quest to remain thin.[75] This 16-year-old girl spends most of her time sweating to at-home workout videos, drinking Diet Coke, and chewing sugar-free gum. So many throwaway lines suggest Cher's grim internalized self-hatred. At the cafeteria, she tells Dionne that "if you cut it like this in little pieces, like really small, you lose weight that way." She connects eating with sin, telling Tai, "I was really bad today, I had two mochaccinos." In an advertisement made specifically for MTV, Cher and Dionne go to the food court and obsessively remove toppings from their Caesar salad until they're left with lemon wedges for lunch. In another MTV promo, a shame-faced Cher delivers a monologue about binge-eating chocolate in the bathroom at a party. Maybe Cher got it from her mom — she died of a "routine liposuction." Through all these scenes and advertisements, Heckerling uses humor to criticize Cher's obsession with her own appearance, and, in turn, the '90's social mandate that girls and women devote their one precious life to becoming

---

75 Unsurprisingly, this thinking was present off-camera, too. Elisa Donovan, who played Amber, has spoken about her debilitating anorexia on the set of *Clueless*.

as small as possible.[76] It's like Heckerling is trying to reach through the screen and say, "This is all a waste of your time! This doesn't matter! It's fucked up!"

All to say, *Clueless* is deeply conscious and critical of some social problems (the culture's pathological need for young girls to hate themselves) and willfully oblivious to others (even a whiff of systemic racism). The movie has selective amnesia, conveniently allowing Heckerling to condemn the issues that apply to her heroine while tabling the social problems that would realistically trouble other characters. To scholar Ayanna Thompson, this "American amnesia" is itself a symptom of a deeper issue: a staunch refusal to actually deal with racial oppression. True, she writes, racism is a challenging subject "and the solutions are neither readily apparent nor easily achievable; so forgetting, while not necessarily natural, is widespread, pervasive, and common." But she also points out that white people are compelled to forget racism in a way that she, as a Black woman, is not.

It serves white people to dismiss these ugly chapters of our history. Doing so alleviates our guilt by brushing our complicity in unimaginable horror under the rug. A "*la la la* I can't hear you" attitude to racial oppression also conveniently leaves white privilege and all its attendant benefits untroubled. For people of color, though, denying the past and present existence of racism must feel like being gaslit. How can one

---

76 Can you tell I had an eating disorder for a decade? Growing up in the '90s and early 2000s was brutal. In high school, every girl I knew hated her body and wanted desperately to fix its endless "problems." What makes me most angry and upset when I look back is that we were *children*. We should have been far too young to internalize such heinous ideas about weight and worth.

group brutally exploit the other for hundreds of years, leave so many of slavery's afterlives firmly in place, then turn around and pout, "Hey, we thought racist stuff back then but now we don't, so stop bringing it up."[77]

This view of racism avoids recognizing that institutions, systems, and even individual people can be discriminatory without being outright bigots. Instead, as in *Clueless*, there's a tacit belief that racism only happens when someone feels prejudice and hatred in their heart. While that's not completely wrong — if a person believes in negative stereotypes, uses slurs, and actively wants an inequitable society based on skin color, then yeah, they're obviously racist — it *is* a conveniently limited way to think about prejudice. According to this scheme, a white person's responsibility to ending racism begins and ends at keeping prejudicial feelings at bay. But that's not enough. We all have a responsibility to end systemic bigotry. As Fannie Lou Hamer said all the way back in 1971, "No one's free until everyone's free."

*Clueless*'s attitude to real-world oppression reminds me a lot of gentrification. The film makes 1995 Los Angeles beautiful and untroubled by benignly, silently displacing potential "trouble" (big scare quotes here because "trouble" is almost always a synonym for people who have a problem with the status quo

---

77 To learn more about how slavery's long shadow continues to impact people of color, I recommend *The New Jim Crow: Mass Incarceration in the Age of Colorblindness* (2010) by Michelle Alexander and *Lose Your Mother: A Journey Along the Atlantic Slave Route* (2006) by Saidiya Hartman.

and all its fuckery). Released three short years after the Los Angeles police were filmed beating Rodney King, Cher and company appear to have no idea that their city hosted one of the most high-profile civil disturbances of the 20th century. Written as America grappled with the AIDS epidemic, the film includes a gay character but none of the queer community's urgent need for support.

This isn't to say that members of marginalized groups are defined only by oppression and pain, but that *Clueless*'s race-and-queerness-blind, happy-go-lucky world is perhaps as skewed as those trauma porn movies that spectacularize suffering.[78] They're both extreme ways of approaching oppression and both leave something to be desired. In the case of *Clueless*, when I sit down and think about race in the film, I'm left feeling cynical — not an emotion I otherwise associate with this hopeful, clever movie. At the end of the day, it seems like Heckerling includes diverse actors to look progressive but then completely ignores a key dimension of their lives. It's toothless.

But all this is a feature, not a bug. Amy Heckerling was not trying to make a documentary or a realistic dramedy about multicultural high schoolers. She was being head-in-the-clouds idealistic. As she said, Bronson Alcott was her "fantasy

---

78 When *12 Years a Slave* (2013) came out, several commentators criticized the movie for seeming to revel in depicting the misery and pain of enslaved Black characters, like Solomon Northup and Patsey. See essays by Carol Boyce Davies, bell hooks, and Armond White. Similar critiques have been made about queer media, specifically the "Bury Your Gays" trope (wherein expendable queer characters die at absurdly higher rates than straight counterparts) and the early 1990s spate of AIDS dramas where gay men are only allowed to be onscreen if they suffer and die.

of what I sort of would have liked everything to be like. Not the way it is. You don't go to high school and see the blacks and whites hanging together and everyone having enough money for nice clothes. That's not the real world, but it would be a nice world." That sounds fair and reasonable — I think most people would agree that a world without racism would be "nice" — but the terms of this idealistic world are telling. Heckerling wants to fast forward to a happy post-race world. She doesn't want to grapple with the work needed to make that happen. In her fantasy, characters of color seamlessly integrate into the reigning world order — one that, as we saw with the whole *Gone with the Wind* debacle, is still coded as subtly hostile.

Remember how Ta-Nehisi Coates defended the movie's treatment of race? Well, he prefaced his comments by saying that Dionne and Murray "just seemed really, really human . . . very, very well-integrated. Very, very believable." In this quote, Coates links three concepts: humanity, integration, believability. I'm a little troubled by this because it suggests that you low-key have to integrate with the reigning order of the day in order to be seen as believably human. In the color-blind world of *Clueless*, what exactly does that integration entail? Based on the movie itself, it seems to mean never bringing up racism. People of color are welcome in *Clueless* — so long as they follow its unspoken rules. The same can be said about how the movie handles homosexuality. Christian can be a visibly gay character who's accepted by straight kids, but only on the condition that he never discuss that part of his life . . . with a girl who's allegedly his friend.[79]

Is this true friendship? I'm not so sure. bell hooks characterizes real friendship as a bond where people are "able to hear honest, critical feedback." If a friendship depends on one party's silence for the other's comfort, then that's not friendship. That kind of relationship sounds more like a parent protecting a child or someone living in fear, cocooning themselves from potential harm. Friendship requires equality and reciprocity, a willingness to listen to each other and care for each other — not a top-down dynamic where one person's voice and ease matters more than the other's. For hooks, "a true friend desires our good." We can't desire a friend's good without understanding their experiences, their history, their life in all its complexity.

When I sit down and think about the friendships in *Clueless*, they end up feeling a little hollow because I don't see this shared desire for each other's good. While Cher's friends help her with her mission to be a better person, Cher is rarely implicated in the larger quest for her friends' wellbeing. She's unchallenged, completely unchagrined by her role in systems

---

79 There's a similar straight-washing to go with the film's tacit white-washing. Forgive me for the following explanation because I will sound like Alice from *The L Word* (2004–2009) working on her intricate chart of lesbian hookups and connections. So, in the original script, the band performing was supposed to be The Breeders, a queer-coded alternative rock group that included the most famous lesbian bassist of the 1990s, Josephine Wiggs. She was in a high-profile relationship with the drummer Kate Schellenbach, another high-profile lesbian musician in the band Luscious Jackson. Luscious Jackson was a big part of the eventual *Clueless* franchise; they appeared on the TV show, their song "Here" was on the original movie's soundtrack, and they even made a tie-in music video with Elisa Donovan and Brittany Murphy. In line with sacred lesbian lore, the setting was a roller derby rink. Anyway, even with all this queer-coded music available, the only live musical performance in the film went to the most het of all genres: White Man with Goatee Appropriates Ska.

that harm her friends. For the writer Christine Pride, whose work often focuses on interracial friendships, the relationship between Cher and Dionne can't count as true intimacy; as she writes, "real friendship means a willingness to listen carefully, and have your views challenged, because your Black friend doesn't see the world the same way you do." Donald Faison, who plays Murray, would agree. When discussing his friendship with *Scrubs* costar Zach Braff in 2020, he argued that the bare minimum for an interracial friendship to survive is for the white friend to accept that "racism is everywhere. It never left. It's always been here . . . Once you don't take that for granted, and you recognize racism is out there, you'll start checking yourself." The fact that our heroine can't even clear this low bar indicts her, her creator, and her historical period.

At least modern viewers can learn from *Clueless*'s grimace-inducing racial politics. They show us how systems of oppression don't just hide in plain sight but are even romanticized as good before our very eyes. By clocking these patterns and tropes in *Clueless*, and popular culture at large, we can recognize the sneaky way that media leads us to internalize and naturalize particular worldviews — most relevant here, the idea that the Black character or the gay character is always the sidekick, never the lead. We're so often told to see media (and especially shiny girly movies like *Clueless*) as politically neutral. They're depicted as a fluffy, harmless escape from real life, but that's just not the case. Popular culture so often *is* ideology by another name. The stories we tell, the tropes we unquestioningly return to — these things subtly reveal our culture's values and ideals. Once we realize this, we can approach pop culture like the philosopher Roland Barthes, who uses mass media as an opportunity to play detective. Through blockbuster films, we can "track down" cultural messages "in the decorative display of what-goes-without-saying."

Dionne is only one in a long and pedigreed line of rom-com besties who deserved better. In honor of our fallen comrades, I've corralled five underserved rom-com BFF character types. If you want to get messy, take a shot whenever I mention a movie with Judy Greer.

THE GAY BEST FRIEND: So ubiquitous as to merit an acronym, the witty, charming GBF regularly overshadows the bland lead. With personality, intellect, and style on retainer, the GBF wins on all fronts. Well, except in the battle for narrative space — the two Dianes, Keaton and Lane, have that in a headlock. One notable and much-deserved exception: Rupert Everett's landmark GBF, George in *My Best Friend's Wedding* (1997), who gets to play knight in shining armor at the end of the movie.

> Additional Examples: Patti (Sandra Oh) in *Under the Tuscan Sun* (2003), Zoe (Frances McDormand) in *Something's Gotta Give*[80] (2003), and Damian (Daniel Franzese and Jaquel Spivey) and Janis (Lizzy Caplan and Auli'i Cravalho) in *Mean Girls* (2004 and 2024).

---

80 I believe the movie includes one line suggesting that this character is straight, but respectfully, no.

THE HORNY SCENE-STEALING KOOK: A dimensional, nuanced personality is nice but not at all necessary in a rom-com. As the name suggests, the Horny Scene-Stealing Kook's three mandated traits are as follows: slutty, funny, and delightful. These BFFs fuck, make jokes, and handily outshine their requisite vanilla besties. They may not be the literal main character, but they're the ones with main character energy. Special shout out to Joan and Bernie in *About Last Night* (2014) — Regina Hall and Kevin Hart have so much damn fun as bickering frenemies who are equal parts hot for and mad at each other (and also mad that they are so hot for each other).

> Additional Examples: Marie (Carrie Fisher) in *When Harry Met Sally* (1989), Delilah (Whoopi Goldberg) in *How Stella Got Her Groove Back* (1998), Casey (Judy Greer!) in *27 Dresses* (2008), Nicole (Mackenzie Davis) and Allan (Adam Driver) in *What If* (2013), and Morgan and Sasha in *Nobody Wants This* (2024–).

THE ZANY LOVABLE CHUB: You know that thing where the Oscars are a little late on an actor's actual best performance, so that when Leonardo DiCaprio wins for *The Revenant* (2015), it's really overdue laurels for, like, *The Wolf of Wall Street* (2013) or one of his many other agro-masc movies? Though lesser known, this also happened to the dearly departed Philip Seymour Hoffman. Technically he won an Oscar for *Capote* (2005), though cinephiles believe this was belated ups for Hoffman's actual greatest performance as ex-child star and basketball sensation Sandy Lyle in *Along Came Polly* (2004). This outrageous man is a pitch-perfect Zany Lovable Chub. He's always up to weird shit, like playing both Judas and Jesus in a community theater production of *Jesus Christ Superstar*, popularizing the term "shart," or inventing endless variations of "make it rain!" while failing to score a single basket. Like St. Sandy, the ZLC has wacky hobbies, endless enthusiasm, and obvious sex appeal to those who know what's good. Only two things keep the Zany Lovable Chub from wholly overpowering their film's comparatively square leads: Hollywood's pathological fatphobia, and the age-old belief that main characters need to be kind of vacuous so that viewers can project themselves onto protagonists. Because of this, the soft, idiosyncratic ZLC is unjustly shuffled to the sidelines — to our collective detriment.

**Additional Examples:** Freddie (John Candy) in *Splash* (1983), Paulette (Jennifer Coolidge) in *Legally Blonde* (2001), Sookie (Melissa McCarthy) in *Gilmore Girls* (2000–2007), Fat Amy (Rebel Wilson) in the *Pitch Perfect* series (2012–2017), and Kelli (Natasha Rothwell) in *Insecure* (2016–2021).

**THE SOUR BRUNETTE:** According to Hollywood, Brown Hair = Killjoy. The Sour Brunette can usually be found dragging down her perky blonde BFF with reality checks or whining about how said BFF is drifting away now that she's got a crush on Troy/Michael/Ben/Bingus. Once aforementioned bestie is paired off with the leading man, The Sour Brunette withers and dies or, worse, receives a pity boyfriend even though she's def coded as a lesbian. Think about Eliza Dushku's Missy in *Bring It On* (2000). Athletic, no-nonsense, and profoundly fine, she spends 90% of the movie telling sweet, simple Torrance (Kirsten Dunst) to get her head out of her ass. The other 10% is spent dancing for Torrance/ stroking Torrance's arm/literally sleeping in the same bed as Torrance. They should be together.

Additional Examples: Vicky (Janeane Garofalo) in *Reality Bites* (1994), Faith (Eliza Dushku) in *Buffy the Vampire Slayer* (1997–2003), Mandella (Susan May Pratt) in *10 Things I Hate About You* (1999), Lilly (Heather Matarazzo) in *The Princess Diaries* (2001), Michelle (Kathryn Hahn) and Jeannie (Annie Parisse) in *How to Lose a Guy in 10 Days* (2003), and Julie (Beanie Feldstein) in *Ladybird* (2017).

JUDY GREER: Girl set the template, making an entire career out of playing rom-com BFFs. In *13 Going on 30* (2004), she's a sleeper cell frenemy. In *27 Dresses* (2008), she performs a sacred rom-com trope: slapping the main character out of a romantic reverie. In *Elizabethtown* (2005), she flexes her muscles by playing not just the hero's salty, long-suffering best friend but his salty, long-suffering *sister*. That's range.

And so on and so forth for *Kissing a Fool* (1998), *Love and Other Drugs* (2010), *Love Happens* (2009), *Playing for Keeps* (2012), and *The Wedding Planner* (2001).

# 6

## I Wanna Help: Comedy and Community

At the end of the day, what does *Clueless* mean? I've spent over 150 pages trying to answer that question. Wallace Shawn, who played curmudgeonly, good-hearted Mr. Hall, only needed a few lines.[81] According to him, the movie is ultimately about "the decency of these characters and the way they do nice things, not really out of principle but more out of instinct." In the world of *Clueless*, "people learn to be more compassionate and nice to each other and understanding of each other, without consciously adopting new principles. This is the meaning of the film." *Clueless*'s significance lies in the characters' innate pull to goodness, their tendency to be kind.

---

81 This footnote is a shameless opportunity for me to tell Wallace Shawn that I'm down to clown. He's so smart and sensual. You see it too, right?

Notice the lack of intent here: Shawn emphasizes that underneath our flaws, our subconscious "instinct" is to be decent. If we could release our death-grip on normativity, we might just be fundamentally good. Could *Clueless* double as the world's most unexpected redemption story?

Ethics, consciousness, absolution — these are *massive* topics, so *Clueless* scales them down to fit the film's fleet runtime. Instead of watching an entire nation progress, Amy Heckerling focuses on a single Los Angeles high school. We see Bronson Alcott go from the usual cliques — AV crew, stoners, "the most popular boys in school" — to a school that *is* one massive friend group. In place of the age-old conflict between an individual and an unjust society, we see Cher battle it out with herself, pivoting from an oblivious queen bee to a budding philanthropist. Instead of wholesale social upheaval, the movie ends with a quieter alternative: a hopeful wedding, symbolizing the triumph of love over hate, life over death, unity over alienation.

One of the things I appreciate most about *Clueless* is that it doesn't just vaguely yearn for a better world. In 90 sparkling minutes, *Clueless* optimistically dramatizes the work it takes to get from where we are now (world on fire) to where we should be (functional, empathetic society symbolized by smiling teens). Because we'd all like to feel more hopeful about life, let's spend a little more time examining how Cher and company got from Point A to Point B.

Basically, we watch Cher Horowitz fail her driver's test, have an epiphany at a fountain, and decide to "makeover

[her] soul." This leads our pert heroine to wonder, "But what makes someone a better person?" The answer is to recognize and contribute to a larger community. Cher figures out what makes a person good by looking at her friends' best qualities and adding her own to the mix. As she says, "All my friends were really good in different ways. Like, Christian, he always wants things to be beautiful and interesting. Or Dionne and Murray, when they think no one is watching, are so considerate of each other." She concludes her internal monologue by reflecting on "poor Miss Geist, always trying to get us involved, no matter how much we resist."

As Cher twiddles her feathery pink pen, Miss Geist tells the class about the Pismo Beach Disaster, a tropical storm that destroyed a neighboring area.[82] Trying to convey the scale of the wreckage, Miss Geist pleads, "Every single possession, every memory, everything you had your whole life — gone in a second. Can you imagine what that must feel like?" Elton raises his hand, leading Miss Geist to look hopeful — maybe a student will care! But of course, he doesn't. Elton remains the personification of navel-gazing, and it turns out that he just wants the hall pass. Undeterred, Miss Geist continues urging the class to get involved with a drive to support those affected by the disaster. The plan is to collect "blankets, disposable diapers, [and] canned goods" to give to people in need. If this had happened earlier in the movie, Cher probably would

---

82 This natural disaster is so named to avoid sounding "dire" according to Heckerling. For what it's worth, when I hear the words Pismo Beach, I think of a bright pink bottle of Pepto Bismol.

have daydreamed through class like any other day. But now that she's been influenced by the goodness of her friends, she decides to do more than the bare minimum. Things are different. Cher raises her hand and says, so simply, so sweetly, "I wanna help." And that's exactly what she does.

As film critic Genevieve Koski writes, Cher's growth lies in the fact that she's finally applying her "interest in helping others, that boundless optimism she's applied to every trifling, petty matter of high-school popularity" to "something outside the narrow sphere of her own life." At last, our heroine looks outward and leverages her enthusiasm, time, and money to help those who really need it. And yes, of course, Cher's change of heart is limited — she ditzily thinks that the Pismo Beach Disaster victims are most in need of caviar and skis — but for Koski and me, that detail makes Cher's redemption realistic, not invalid. For a sheltered 16-year-old, she's doing all right.

In the happy logic of a fairy tale or fable, we immediately see the fruits of Cher's labor, the just reward for her change of heart. Students flock to her booth about the relief drive. Boxes overflow with donations for the cause, sorted by Cher into "entrées and appetizers." Lovable skater Travis Birkenstock, currently working through a 12-step program, drops by to donate some bongs (to the kitchenware section — bless). In the process, he and Cher become friends, which also paves the way for Cher's reconciliation with Tai.

Like a hop, skip, and a jump, we nimbly move from this renewed friendship to Cher and Josh beginning a romantic relationship to the life-affirming wedding of Miss Geist and Mr. Hall, attended by our six luminous main characters — Cher, Josh, Dionne, Murray, Tai, Travis. Ditz, tree-hugger, fashionista, brace-face, alt girl, and grunge skater unite to celebrate the small miracle of two people falling in love. The cerulean and lime green credits roll. A narrator might as well declare that they all lived happily ever after.

*Clueless* is so well situated in the self-aware, and often cynical, 1990s that it may surprise you to learn about its roots in centuries-old comedic tropes and strategies. According to scholars of humor, even silly jokes are surprisingly revolutionary. By upending basic assumptions, they subtly challenge the status quo. Old-school literary critics extend this thinking by arguing that classic comedy is all about taking a flawed society and transforming it into a more egalitarian, forward-thinking social order. Given deepening inequality in the real world, comedies may have a lot to teach us about troubling the status quo and fostering our own communities — actions that, according to bell hooks, do nothing less than "sustain life" itself. Without feeling preachy or phony, *Clueless* doubles as both a comfort watch and a crash course for viewers hoping to improve themselves and their world.

In its oldest sense, "comedy" refers to a play where the main characters are genuinely good, well-intentioned people who make mistakes because of poor judgment, not malice or evil. Over the course of the story, characters who did shitty things recognize that they were wrong and grow from their mistakes. In the final pages, everyone unites and enjoys a collective happy ending; reconciliation rules the day. Social harmony is usually symbolized through a wedding or a big party, some kind of occasion where everyone gets together and has fun.[83]

Though all this sounds sweet and nice, comedy does not always equal escapism or a pie-in-the-sky reprieve from real-life problems. There is more going on here, as literary critics have insisted for literally thousands of years. In Ancient Greece, the poet Horace famously urged writers to "instruct and delight" — to use entertaining stories as Trojan Horses for moral lessons. So yes, comedies are fun, but like any other form of literature, they can also teach us important things. For example, in the Ancient Greek comedy *Lysistrata* (411 BC), Aristophanes writes about wives who use a sex strike to make their husbands stop fighting pointless wars. Jokes abound about everyone's thirst, but the bigger lesson still stands: War, what is it good for? Something similar happens in plenty of Shakespearean comedies. In *As You Like It* (approx. 1599) and *Twelfth Night* (approx. 1601), women cross-dress as men, which leads to entertaining chaos, plus a pointed criticism of the het world order. Channelling Dionne here, Horace would "kvell."

---

83 Much modern comedy — rom-coms, coming-of-age movies, sitcoms — stays true to this template, but to accommodate other directions in the genre (satire, dramedy, dark comedy), the definition of comedy has expanded to broadly mean amusing, humorous entertainment that makes the audience laugh. For example, *Veep* (2012–2019) is hilarious but almost every character is terrible, and at the end the group gathers at main character Selina Meyers's deeply underwhelming funeral, rather than a buoyant wedding. All to say, funny shows can be comedies without fulfilling all the genre's original elements, like a focus on making up and growing for the better.

Fast forward a few centuries and we find a Canadian academic homing in on just how comedies manage this balancing act. The literary scholar Northrop Frye argued that comedy "instructs" us by helping us imagine our ideal society and then test-driving ways we might create such a world. If a comedy does its job right, when the curtain falls, the audience will feel profound relief because the happy ending will depict the world as it should be. To Frye, classic comedies (like plays by Aristophanes and Shakespeare) are like myths. They're symbolic stories that give us a peek into a world we desire and see as intrinsically right. When the cast takes a bow after a play like *Much Ado About Nothing* (approx. 1598), the audience steps back in awe and says, "Oh yes, that's it. That's what we've been trying to get at over here in the real world. Reconciliation, harmony, generosity: That's what it's all about."

Importantly, Frye doesn't pitch this kind of world as an impossible ideal that we can never reach. Instead, he insists that this happy, harmonious place is the world's "genuine" form.[84] A functional, generous society is something to which we're inclined. It's attainable, authentic. If we tabled all the bullshit, the world would default to decency. This is why I find Frye's idea of comedy so hopeful. It pitches humanity as *already* inclined to goodness. Yes, we have flaws (boy howdy, do we), but that's because we're wayward and juvenile, not because we're hopeless failures or evil monsters. This is a gentler, more

---

84 Here's Frye's full quote: "Shakespearean comedy illustrates as clearly as any mythos we have, the archetypal function of literature in visualizing the world of desire, not as an escape from 'reality,' but as the genuine form of the world that human life tries to imitate." I really love this idea!

optimistic way to see the world: Things aren't great yet but give it time. We'll get there. We'll figure it out.

Remember how classic comedies always end with a party or wedding? In *Clueless*, Amy Heckerling nods to this generic convention when Miss Geist and Mr. Hall get hitched. True, in a Shakespearean comedy, two young hots would walk down the aisle and replace their fusty parents as the new leaders in town. But even though our young characters aren't the literal bride and groom (as Cher says, "As if! I'm only 16 and this is California, not Kentucky"), the camera focuses on Cher, Josh, Dionne, Murray, Tai, and Travis far more than their teachers.[85] Plus, the final shot is of Cher and Josh kissing. This all suggests that the youths are the ones who matter at this wedding. These are the kids who will continue *Clueless*'s cheery commitment to a brighter, more egalitarian society.

Like so much of the movie, the wedding scene is lit with bright sunshine. We're outside with flowers in bloom, in a verdant green world bursting with life. As General Public's irresistible song "Tenderness" plays, the audience enjoys one final moment in the world of *Clueless* — a world characterized by optimism, goodness, and happiness. Artists involved in the film were committed to this vision.

Amy Heckerling described the world of the movie as a "happy, youthful, optimistic place where somebody can see

---

85  Amber, Elton, and Christian are also in attendance! They don't sit at the same table as the six lead characters but they're visible in the audience.

what's good in people and what's good in the world." Production designer Steve Jordan based the film's bright visual style on one word: *happiness*. Jordan's mission was to make the movie "a place they [the audience] want to be." I think they succeeded. I would love to go on a vacation to *Clueless* Land.

Part of why this world feels so inviting is because it also feels fully realized. If you watch the movie with an eye on the background, you'll notice that there's always a ton going on, especially in scenes set at Bronson Alcott High School. Here's a fun example: A bunch of girls have bandaged noses early in the film. It's never commented on, but it's Heckerling's subtle dig at Beverley Hills teenagers who time their nose jobs to heal by prom. Similarly, extras are dressed meticulously by costume designer Mona May.[86] She intentionally made sure that *Clueless* wasn't going to be a movie where the main characters look amazing and everyone else looks like garbage. If you keep an eye out for Cher's classmates, you'll see wacky hair styles (space buns!), distinctive clothing, and weird props. One girl in a bright patchwork jacket uses a blue highlighter like it's lip gloss. A trio exchange manicure supplies during homeroom. There's a funny refrain where students wear nonsensical neon earmuffs in stereotypical California weather.

Across the board, there's a conspicuous effort to include background characters in the film's optimistic world. It's not that this attention makes the world feel real; straight-up realism was never *Clueless*'s interest, and true to form, these kids are

86 Justice for Mona May. She designed costumes for *Clueless* (1995), *Romy and Michele's High School Reunion* (1997), and *Enchanted* (2007). Where is her Oscar?

dressed more like characters in a Dr. Seuss book than actual 1990s teens. It's more that this effort develops the imagined, fantastical world of the film. There's a visual richness here. You feel like you could walk right in, like this over-the-top movie could be a magical portal to a better, brighter world. There's a lovely sense of attention and inclusion on display here — a sustained interest in how community enriches the world.[87]

Shot composition enhances this message, too. Amy Heckerling and Steve Jordan collaborated to compose shots that include multiple characters onscreen at a time. In a conversation scene, for instance, the camera will often film characters sitting or standing side by side rather than cutting back and forth between individual shots of isolated talking heads. We see this all over the movie — when Cher and Josh bicker on the sofa, when Dionne and Murray share a sandwich, when Tai and Cher reconcile after their fight, and on and on.

When the movie *does* use a more fragmented, individualistic shot, it's often in scenes of distress and conflict: when Elton aggressively hits on Cher after the party in the Valley, when Cher is robbed at gunpoint, when the driving examiner tells Cher she failed. There's a clear association here: Things go poorly when a community is fractured into antagonistic

---

87 Ever since I saw *Lady Bird* (2017), I can't think of the word *attention* without thinking of the lovely exchange between the guidance counselor Sister Sarah Joan and our heroine Lady Bird. Sister Sarah Joan tells Lady Bird that the way she writes about Sacramento makes it clear that she loves her hometown. Lady Bird, who can't wait to leave, is confused: "Sure, I guess I pay attention." Then Sister Sarah Joan asks, "Don't you think maybe they are the same thing? Love and attention?" When we take time to truly consider something, to attend to it, I do think that's a form of love. (Also, hello to my poor, long-suffering partner, Mitch, who has dealt with an attention-deficit spouse for the better part of a decade. Sorry I can't practice what I preach! I'm trying! Please remember that I am also very cute!)

individuals. We inhabit a much warmer, happier world when characters share the frame, share their time, and share themselves with each other. This kind of shot is the default in *Clueless* — being together is the movie's home base.

On a formal level, then, *Clueless* requires viewers to see people as belonging to larger communities. We're not islands, floating by ourselves — and indeed when characters are alone, that's a sign that something's gone wrong. In a million subtle ways, *Clueless* argues that we need each other, that things get better when people unite. Again, though, we find ourselves facing a contradiction where this is both nice to think and hard to see actually happening. As always, the world of *Clueless* is both aspirational and comfortable. We want this harmonious world precisely because we *don't* have it yet, *and* we feel at home in this good place because, as Frye would say, it's where we naturally belong.

According to *Clueless*, transforming a shitty world to a less shitty world involves nurturing empathy and charity, resolving conflicts, and committing to friendship. Rocket science this is not. But the phrase "easier said than done" certainly comes to mind when I write these abstract concepts down. We all know that these qualities are good, but making time to cultivate them is another story. Tackling the inertia of the status quo — the immobilization accompanied by thoughts like *I have a million other things to do* or *me being nicer won't change anything structural* — this is the internal work that needs to be done in order to move forward to tangible, on-the-ground, local community building, like the Pismo Beach Disaster Relief effort.

In a recent book, author and activist Casey Plett concludes that despite all the complexities and contradictions of community, at the end of the day, the most important thing is to get out there and *do something*. Her final anecdote remembers a day where she blew off work to attend a Trans Ladies Picnic. Again, like Cher captaining the relief drive, this is not full metal social revolution. But! It matters. Plett quotes the poet Tracy K. Smith as saying, "Every seismic social shift originates in someone's kitchen or living room with the decision to cease doing something that only recently had felt perfectly normal, or to accept the necessity of an action that had seemed impossible, unthinkable." For Plett, going to a picnic fulfills this brief: "It felt so impossible that afternoon to call in and go to that picnic, but I did." She concludes with these words: "What else can I do now that seems unthinkable? And what about you? Don't give up on it. Don't give up on this stuff."

Little moments matter. They matter in and of themselves and they matter because they can spur further action. [88] When Smith writes about the "seismic" changes wrought by a change of perspective in a kitchen, she's also writing about the fight for Black liberation. When Plett writes about the picnic, she's writing about the bigger work of forging transgender community — carving out a place for trans joy, friendship, and connection in a world that so often punishes these human needs.

88 Though obviously I would be concerned if social justice began and ended with the 1% sometimes helping with a food drive.

It's obviously imperfect to bring a rich white girl at a food drive into a conversation about these larger real-world struggles, but it *is* worth pointing out that *Clueless* also moves from a specific context (Pismo Beach Disaster Relief) to a broader social message. Cher literally clears out her litigator dad's mansion so that people who need things can have them. The food drive is baby's first experiment with redistributing the wealth.

These moral messages are all positive rather than negative. Instead of tut-tutting and telling viewers what *not* to do, Plett, Smith, and, yes, even Heckerling are interested in what *can* be done to make things better. This connects back to comedy as a genre. The philosopher Simon Critchley has argued that humor reveals "the depths of what we share." The literary critic William Empson admires pastoral comedy's "unifying social force." Northrop Frye celebrates how comedy ends with scenes of communion that reach out beyond the characters and into the audience. This is such a wonderful and, I think, necessary change of pace from dire art about how miserable and alone we all are. A film like *Clueless* ends so much more constructively. It invites viewers to join the party, to commit to building a positive community in the real world. This is *Clueless*'s great power. Heckerling's good-hearted comedy urges viewers to develop a kinder, more equitable society by getting out there and helping people who could use a hand.

All that said, I also think — as I've made clear throughout this book — that *Clueless* is a product of its time. Its ideas about an "ideal" society are inevitably different than our preferences today. Taken constructively, this means that we can recognize the ending as an oh-so-1990s vision of utopia, with all the limitations that entails. It's not lost on me that the movie's proposal for an improved society contains some deeply regressive ideas. All the couples at the end of the film are sorted into tidy demographics. Two middle-class teachers marry. Two of the film's few Black characters end up together. Tai and Travis, both from lower-income families, are paired off. And then, of course, the rich kids get together. There are no interclass couples (as we already know, that idea gets shut down hard by Cher when Tai develops a crush on Josh). There's not even the possibility of interracial romantic love (the TV show continues this strain — over three seasons, Cher never entertains the possibility of a boyfriend who isn't white).

It's a very white, 1990s perspective on diversity and inclusion: one that refuses to recognize race or class based on the allegedly well-intentioned idea that "we're all the same" that stuff "doesn't matter." But of course, by failing to consider the complex and oppressive histories of these categories, the movie just ends up perpetuating the vagaries of both systems. There is clearly a demarcated place where Dionne and Tai are allowed to be — and it's below Cher. At the end of the movie, which so often pokes fun at Cher's insulated, limited perspective, Heckerling winds up buying into what she previously troubled. Cher's happy-go-lucky view of the world — which we know can be limited to the point of ignorance — is the one the film prefers in its final frames.

In an alternate universe where I could pitch a *Clueless* remake or sequel to people with money in Hollywood, I'd try to amend this problem. The film ends with Cher discovering how important it is to help others, so, duh, the next chapter should detail her burgeoning work as an activist. After all, actual protestors held signs quoting Cher's debate speech on Haitian refugees ("It does not say *RSVP* on the Statue of Liberty") at demonstrations against Donald Trump's hostile "Muslim ban," a 2017 executive order that harshly restricted immigration from Iran, Iraq, Libya, Somalia, Sudan, Syria, and Yemen. Given the film's overall arc *and* real-world fan response to Cher's story, it makes sense that a continuation of the film could focus on Cher and Josh attending protests, lobbying for legal change, and organizing aid.

Instead, in actual adaptations of *Clueless*, including a network television show and an off-Broadway jukebox musical starring Dove Cameron, the writers simply reset Cher to the beginning of the original film. Apparently, the audience interested in *Clueless* spin-offs, remakes, and continuations wants to see Cher learn to be nice — but only up to a certain point of political activity. In the film's original script, this means that Cher participates in a blood drive. In the final movie, we hit this limit with the Pismo Beach Disaster Relief. The off-Broadway musical follows suit by replicating the donation drive; the main difference is adding a (tongue in cheek?) rendition of the New Radicals's "You Get What You Give."[89] The TV show, which ran

---

89  Choice lyrics include "We're flat broke / But hey, we do it in style / The bad rich / God's flying in for your trial."

from 1996 to 1999 on ABC, has a few variations on this theme. Across three seasons, Cher and friends clean up a city park, invite a working-class man to Thanksgiving dinner, and give a poor girl named Casey a makeover. In that episode, Casey asks Cher, Dionne, and Amber why they have "everything" when she has "nothing." Cher replies by explaining that "money isn't everything." Casey's dad loves her, which means that where it counts, she's just as rich as Cher and her friends. Woof.

There's also an unhinged episode called "We Shall Overpack," where Cher leads a walkout to protest a backpack ban. Throughout, the episode equivocates the Civil Rights Movement, the 1976 South African student uprising, and the Tiananmen Square Protests with Bronson Alcott students' need to accessorize. At one point, Cher addresses the student body and riffs on Martin Niemöller's famous speech criticizing Nazism. Her version goes, "First they came for my backpack, and I did not speak." Obviously, the episode plays all this as a bathetic joke. It's objectively insane for Cher to think these issues are on the same level. The punchline doesn't criticize protesting as stupid; the target is Cher's juvenile belief that her "struggles" come anywhere near the unrest she learns about in class. So, yes, I understand what the episode is trying to do. But it's still hard to watch without wincing given the show's total silence on anything resembling contemporary social issues. You can't have it both ways.

I only got more uncomfortable as the episode wrapped up. In the final minutes, Cher proclaims that she is now an activist. The next issue she will tackle is, get ready, the school colors.

She's going to stump for pastels for spring and earth tones for fall. I find this ending dispiriting because, once again, we see that recursive loop. Cher seems to learn and grow, only for her mindset to reset to the beginning of the original film. Even after learning the same lesson again and again, she remains well-intentioned but ignorant.

What's up with these half-baked politics? Why do adaptations shy away from the most heartening elements of the movie's *actual* ending? Why is there a concrete wall blocking Cher's further development?[90] Well, companies want to sell merch, so potentially alienating half your audience along party lines isn't a savvy sales strategy. If you bring in activism, it must be a bland, centrist issue, ideally something related to the environment (Josh is part of TreePeople) or a natural disaster (*ding ding ding*, Pismo Beach!). Plus, it's not like the actual movie really pushed the envelope in its treatment of identity — in considering anything too close to the fraught terrain of race and class to be third rail, the TV show and musical stay uncomfortably close to their source material. And then there's the general reluctance to pivot from entertainment to an afternoon special. I understand this: Most of the time, when TV shows and movies do edutainment, I feel less like I've learned something and more like I've watched a massive corporation give itself a pat on the back.

---

90 Dystopian metatextual adaptation idea: a *Clueless* horror film where Cher is continually looped back in time to relearn the same lessons over and over until they stick.

Luckily for us, one genre has a built-in escape hatch to the dangers of overly simple and serious social commentary: comedy. Comedy can use cleverness and humor to explore and defang huge social problems. In fact, coyly fighting the power is one of the genre's bigger commitments. According to the anthropologist Mary Douglas, humor overturns our expectations. Comedy provides an opportunity to realize "that an accepted pattern has no necessity." This is the joy of a joke: We hear a prompt and are delighted when the answer is unlike anything we imagined. The link between cause and effect is broken in an exuberant way. Common sense has left the building. This can be a supremely freeing attitude — especially if we extend this thinking to society.

The philosopher Simon Critchley argues that humor can disrupt the powers that be by revealing that the social rules we live by are, well, kind of fake. They're just a story that we believe in. If we decide that we don't believe in those norms anymore, or see that those rules no longer serve us, then we can just as easily revoke our belief. "By laughing at power," Critchley explains, "we expose its contingency, we realize that what appeared to be fixed and oppressive is in fact the emperor's new clothes, and just the sort of thing that should be mocked and ridiculed." If authority depends on our belief for its power, the theory goes, we can simply . . . take that belief away. As easily as we bought into this system, we can flip the script.

Laughter's challenge to tradition is part of why feminist scholars often interpret comedy as "a genre of resistance, upheaval, and change," a genre that "expands what is possible." The academic Kathleen Rowe uses the classic drag comedy *Some*

*Like It Hot* (1959) to support this idea. It's a beloved movie from the 1950s that ends with a gay marriage. How does it get away with this? Comedy. It's like the Old Hollywood equivalent of the "joking . . . unless?" meme. Because there's plausible deniability (it's just a joke!), writers can get away with provocative messages.

Imagine if a sequel or remake of *Clueless* modernized the original's satire and saw it through to a more satisfying conclusion. I would love to watch Emma Seligman (writer/director of the instant classic *Bottoms* [2023]) take this on, maybe with Hunter Schafer as Cher and Zendaya as Dionne. They could lead a high school revolution powered by Gen Z's bone-dry humor. Or, what if Karyn Kusama drew on her background in horror to retell the movie from Tai's perspective, complete with a takedown of Cher as queen bee and the busted social hierarchy she represents? Ziwe could write a funny, wry adaptation where Dionne takes center stage as a rare Black ditz. And even though this idea might be sacrilege to folks who think *Clueless* has to de facto center a girl's perspective, I would be very down for a version where Murray and Sean (Sean Holland, whose character is vastly expanded from the original movie in the TV series) become our wry main characters. These two are absolute lights in the otherwise mediocre TV show.[91]

91 In one of the bananas episodes I mentioned before, they provide the only reasonable lines of dialogue. Cher and Dionne declare that they are planning a revolution to combat the backpack ban. Murray replies, "You know, Sean, it is so refreshing to see such passion from our youth. Forget poverty, crumbling infrastructure, our overtaxed healthcare system. You guys are absolutely right, a fashion statement is an issue of global importance." In another episode where Cher and Dionne wear teddy bear backpacks and say they're a fashion statement, Murray provides a characteristically verbose takedown: "Cher, the only statement they're making is the primal scream against the loss of childhood, a deep-rooted fear of adult responsibilities, and the atavistic yearning for simpler times. You know this." Donald Faison has the best dialogue in the series.

And why limit ourselves to straightforward storytelling in the first place? Netflix has experimented with interactive film and TV, most famously with the "Bandersnatch" (2018) episode of *Black Mirror* (2011–). A Choose Your Own Adventure *Clueless* adaptation could tease out these bigger questions by giving viewers an arena to test-drive their own ideas about how this classic movie could shift for a new audience. Given *Clueless*'s interest in community, wouldn't it make sense for a modern adaptation to reach out to the viewer and ask for their input?

At the end of a comedy, "something gets born." That's Northrop Frye's language and it stands out because he's usually not a clunky writer. (For an academic, he's actually a *really* good writer in that I can mostly understand what he's trying to say without wanting to eat my own head.) But I'll give him a pass because, as usual, he's right. At the end of the day, classic comedy is creative. These are stories that imagine what *could* happen and then work to make it so. They combine a daydreamy reveling in possibility, hopefulness, and optimism, with a more clear-eyed interest in how characters could develop such goodness. What's more, in comedy, pursuing a more just society does not have to be characterized by endless doom-and-gloom struggle. Building a better world involves error, for sure, but for the most part this is joyous work, full of laughter and goodwill.

If it plays by the rules of the genre, a classic comedy's final moments celebrate the arrival of a better world. We kind of achieve this at the end of *Clueless*. Bronson Alcott High School still isn't perfect — not by a long shot — but it is better. Things have improved and that's not nothing. Incremental change is still change. The task at this point is to avoid the pitfalls of official continuations like the TV show and off-Broadway musical. We can't just keep repeating the same lesson over and over. That would mean we haven't learned our lesson at all.

We all know it's only a matter of time until a disappointing *Clueless* remake drops. But until that day comes, we can dream of myriad, sometimes unhinged, always unlikely-to-be-bankrolled-by-a-big-studio futures for our friends at Bronson Alcott High School. Figure out your preferred riff on Cher's story with the quiz below. Keep track of your answers as you go through!

1. What's your favorite genre?

   A) Black comedy

   B) Feel-good teen movie

   C) Paranoid thriller

   D) Romantic comedy

   E) Fizzy musical

2. Choose your ideal adaptation style.

   A) Retelling from the villain's point of view. I want the *Clueless* equivalent of *Wide Sargasso Sea* (1966) or *Wicked* (1995).

   B) Minimal alterations — remakes should stay true to the source material.

   C) Straightforward sequel. Tell me what happens after the first movie ends.

   D) Straightforward prequel. Give me the backstory.

   E) Surprise me! The weirder, the better.

3. Which *Clueless* character do you most identify with?

   A) An unholy meld of Tai and Mr. Hall

   B) Cher, duh

   C) Sweet, socially responsible Josh

   D) Dionne and/or Murray and/or their bickering

   E) Justice for Ms. Stoeger

4. What's your preferred plotline?

   A) Fiery social revolution!

   B) A girly take on the classic coming-of-age tale

   C) Investigators unearth and expose corruption

   D) Funny, swoon-worthy love story

   E) Story of self-discovery via unlikely romance

5. Which double bill are you most likely to see?

   A) *Heathers* (1988) followed by *Dude, Where's My Car?* (2000)

   B) *Clueless* (1995) followed by *Clueless* (1995)

   C) *Sneakers* (1992) followed by *Dick* (1999)

   D) *The Proposal* (2009) followed by *Rye Lane* (2023)

   E) *The Adventures of Priscilla, Queen of the Desert* (1994)
      followed by *The Incredibly True Adventure of Two Girls
      in Love* (1995)

6. What's your favorite *Clueless* quote/scene?

   A) "Thank you, thank you. This is so unexpected. I
      didn't even have a speech prepared. But I would like

to say this: Tardiness is not something you can do all on your own. Many, many people had to contribute to my tardiness. I'd like to thank my parents for never driving me to school, the L.A. bus drivers for taking a chance on an unknown kid, and last, but not least, the wonderful crew at McDonald's for the long hours they spend making Egg McMuffins, without which I might never be tardy. Thank you."

B) "I totally paused."

C) "May I please remind you that it does not say *RSVP* on the Statue of Liberty."

D) "My plastic surgeon doesn't want me doing any activity where balls fly at my nose." "Well, there goes your social life."

E) "Searching for a boy in high school is as useless as searching for meaning in a Pauly Shore movie."

7. Which chapter in this book intrigued you most?

A) "Way Harsh: Class and Tension"

B) "A Ditz with a Credit Card: Innocence and Ignorance"

C) "I Wanna Help: Comedy and Community"

D) A tie between "Excuse Me, Miss Dionne: Love" and "Not to Your Face: Friendship and Silence"

E) N/A — I'm here for the deranged interludes and footnotes

Count up your answers and consult the answer key for your ideal *Clueless* adaptation.

MOSTLY A'S: Tai Frasier takes center stage in this adaptation which melds stoner comedy and *Les Mis*–esque social revolution. When Tai arrives at a glossy Beverly Hills high school, she struggles to balance a part-time job at one of LA's 40,000 dispensaries, a flirtationship with a precious skater named Travis, and brutal commutes courtesy of unreliable city buses. Her debate teacher, Mr. Hall, keeps penalizing her for excessive tardies until Tai delivers a presentation explaining the connection between low-income households and educational disadvantage. Mr. Hall sees the light and joins Tai as she leads a working-class revolution at Bronson Alcott. Perks of this adaptation include a 100% increase in Wallace Shawn screen time and improved class commentary.

MOSTLY B'S: These were trick options. You don't want an adaptation; you want to rewatch *Clueless* for the nth time. This is never a bad idea so please go forth and enjoy. If, after your viewing, you want to learn about your second-choice adaptation, retake this quiz and don't choose any B's, xoxo.

MOSTLY C'S: In this sequel, Cher, Dionne, and Tai continue to develop their interest in social justice via a wackadoo plotline where the girls overhear one of Mel's work calls and figure out he's involved in some shady shit. The trio and their boyfriends band together to take down Mel's law firm — I'm imagining scenes where they break into their offices under cover of night, discover the dark backstory of "the September 3rd call," and redistribute the ill-gotten Horowitz fortune. Perks of this adaptation: We *finally* get a *Clueless* continuation where Cher doesn't just reset to the beginning of the movie, plus more Dan Hedaya screaming at people is always a good thing.

MOSTLY D'S: This prequel is *The Godfather Part II* (1974) to *Clueless*'s *The Godfather* (1972). The record scratch, freeze frame, "you're probably wondering how I got here" backstory that we both need and deserve. I give you: Dionne and Murray's love story. In this sweet rom-com, viewers will learn how a goofball like Murray won over a queen like Dionne. Here's what I'm thinking: Dionne's dating her ideal guy as specified in the scene at the mall restaurant (on a buff waiter: "Too puny. I like 'em big"): an oafish jock who's physically attractive but mentally lacking, i.e., any of the himbos in my "Key to All Mythologies: Airhead Edition" interlude. He abruptly breaks up with her to focus on gains, leading a wounded Dionne to panic about the upcoming dance. To make her ex jealous, she and her old friend Murray start fake dating, but as time goes on, they realize that they're really falling for each other. Perks of this adaptation: two excellent rom-com tropes (Friends to Lovers *and* Fake Dating) plus a nice inversion of the Black Best Friend trope. In this adaptation, Cher's the sidekick to Dionne.

MOSTLY E'S: Okay, so I didn't have a natural place to put this in the book, but I am into the minor internet theory that Cher is a lipstick lesbian dealing with compulsory heterosexuality. Evidence: She falls for a gay guy, she rarely seems physically attracted to the men she purports to like, and she can't drive.[92] (Between the flannel and Tai's declaration that she's "never had straight friends before," I don't think I even need to make a case that Tai's at least bisexual.) With this foundation in place, this off-the-wall musical adaptation of *Clueless* would set Cher's queer coming of age to contemporary covers of canonical lesbian-approved songs. We'd get a sweet, slow burn love story between a richy rich kid and a grungy soft butch from the wrong side of the tracks, plus Ms. Stoeger would give Cher a big "go get the girl!" speech in the last half hour. Perks of this adaptation: *Clueless* could fully lean into queer-coded camp plus *imagine* how good the soundtrack would be. Janelle Monáe covering "All the Things She Said"? Hayley Kiyoko reworking "The Weakness in Me"?! Tegan and Sara's version of "Come to My Window"??!! I'd die.

---

92 I'm allowed to make this joke because I'm queer (and, playing to type, a terrible driver).

# 7

## I Have Direction: Coda

It may surprise you to learn, in this age of inescapable franchises and transmedia brand expansions, that the original *Clueless* film was just that: a film. In 1995, *Clueless* stayed true to its satire of vacuous materialism by avoiding tie-in merch. Well, except for one pocket book called *Cher's Guide to . . . Whatever* (1995) and (obviously) the VHS tape. Beyond that, viewers in search of *Clueless* swag were out of luck. You couldn't buy *Clueless*-themed clothing, feathery pink pens, stickers, or anything else because it simply didn't exist.

Until 1997. When the TV show came out on ABC that year, the *Clueless* brand's previous restraint disappeared into thin air. ABC worked with clothing store Wet Seal on a fashion line inspired by the new show, publishing house Simon & Schuster on a young adult novel series, and toy behemoth Mattel on

Cher, Dionne, and Amber Barbies, among other licensing deals. From this point, the genie couldn't go back into the bottle. The *Clueless*-inspired "Fancy" music video by Iggy Azalea and Charli XCX featured obvious product placement for Revolve clothing, a massive fast fashion website. Brands like Clean Lines, Hot Topic, Old Navy, and Walmart have all partnered with Paramount for uninspired *Clueless* T-shirts. Alicia Silverstone has reprised her signature role as Cher in advertisements for designer clothing and a cash back shopping platform. Again and again, *Clueless*'s cleverness is reduced to cute outfits and shopping sprees.

It's more than a little hypocritical for companies to monetize *Clueless* — a movie that clearly skewers materialism — but also unavoidable given our current capitalist hellscape. Fast fashion *Clueless* T-shirts are a way for corporations to, as always, integrate and neutralize potential threats. By defanging a film that critiques overconsumption, *Clueless* gets safely looped back into the culture it tried to satirize. Someone wryly wearing a *Clueless* sweatshirt — even if they know full well that the original movie side-eyed commercialism — is just the girly version of a mass-produced Misfits tee. Unfortunately for *Clueless* and punk fans alike, it's hard to signal your allegiance to anti-establishmentarianism without the infrastructure of the establishment.[93]

And anyway, all this makes perfect sense because of course these companies aren't trying to endorse *Clueless*'s critique of

93 Potential girls' night in activity to solve this problem: Host a clothing swap and watch *Clueless* while DIYing Riot-grrrl-aesthetic secondhand *Clueless* tees. You know mine would say "Ugh, as if!"

materialism in the first place. They're trying to sell stuff —
and they're succeeding thanks to one simple trick. Companies
stimulate their customers' nostalgia, their sentimental longing
for a time that has come and gone.

When I stumble upon a *Clueless*-themed sticker or a yellow
plaid jacket, the nostalgia rush kicks in hard. I feel a giddy
thrill as my brain and my heart revisit not just the movie, but
all the emotions and associations that the movie holds for me.
I don't remember the exact first time I saw *Clueless*, but I know
I saw it when I was young. Just because of that, I automatically
associate the movie with the joy of childhood, obviously seen
through rose-colored glasses. When I think about *Clueless*, I
think about growing up in the 1990s with all its deliciously
tacky fashion and girl power craze, about sugar-fueled movie
nights with my sister, about feeling fucking fabulous as I wore
the lime green platform sneakers that my mom and I scored at
Zellers (on sale!). Like a shopaholic angel watching over me,
*Clueless* is in the background of all these lovely memories and
many more.

When my teenage self discovered Jane Austen and went
ham for 19th-century novels, I remember being blown away
by the fact that one of my favorite comfort watches was also
a secret Austen adaptation. Way too late into my undergrad
degree, I *finally* realized that the art my boyfriends liked wasn't
necessarily good, it was just made for boys. If they could own
their cultural milieu, so could I own mine. *Clueless* was one of
the first girly girl movies I plastered over my Facebook page —
a small gesture, yes, but nevertheless a turning point in my

development as a scholar and a person. A step on my way to curating an internal world that aligned with my own values rather than the ones I'd been conditioned to see as worth my time. A choice in favor of optimism, generosity, hopefulness, good-heartedness, cleverness, critical thinking, and unabashed femininity.

Look at that. In just two paragraphs, I've fallen headfirst into the nostalgia trap. It's so easy to go from imagining merch to reminiscing about the past to waxing rhapsodic about your entire life — and, as you may have noticed, constructing a tidy little story about who you are, where you've come from, and how those experiences have influenced the person you are today. In the last page or so, without intending to, I wound up writing a very, very condensed memoir about how girly art has shaped my life. Of course, that story is nowhere near encompassing the actual messiness of my life. It's half a dozen cherry-picked anecdotes that support my thesis: that my life has an arc, a shape, a comprehensible meaning. That I exist, that my time on Earth is meaningful to someone, even if it's just myself.

This is part of what nostalgia does, according to David Berry, who wrote an entire book on the feeling. In *On Nostalgia* (2020), Berry argues that nostalgia "makes us feel like ourselves." To be nostalgic is to yearn for the "authentic" — to reconnect with a vision of ourselves that feels true, to return to a time where things made more sense. But of course, we can't really go back. And even if we could, it wouldn't be satisfying. The objective reality would feel like a slap in the face compared to the rosy memories we've shaded in over years and years of reminiscing.

At this point, as our hypothetical shopper, I'm feeling stuck. This little item — be it a sticker, a T-shirt, a *Clueless*-inflected blazer — has brought up so many bittersweet memories and impossible desires that I'm left with a longing that can never be satisfied. I guess the second-best thing will have to do. I pick up the sticker and walk to the cash register. While tapping my credit card, I feel both euphoric and relieved. All those contradictory, insatiable feelings have been exorcised in the act of buying some merch. Retail therapy indeed.

I understand why companies use nostalgia to sell stuff: because it works. Nostalgia and consumerism are two sides of the same coin. Both stoke overwhelming feelings of desire that can only be temporarily satisfied — if they can be satisfied at all. Wait a few hours, days, or maybe even weeks, and there it is, that yearning all over again. When it comes to consumerism, this system works perfectly. We see a product that connects with us, a product that we don't need yet find ourselves wanting. The product tells us a story (I can fix you, I can take you back to a simpler time, I can reveal you to yourself) and in purchasing the product, we also buy relief. We've sated our larger existential debt. But because this gratification is — by design — short of what we really require, the loop inevitably begins all over again. We're never truly satisfied, which keeps the wheels of commerce turning.

This may sound like a familiar idea, even if it's dressed up in more academic language. After all, it's the central argument of *Clueless*. Cher has everything money can buy — a Jeep with a monster sound system, a house with three separate fireplaces (that we can see — there could be more), and a closet so large that the term *closet* doesn't really suffice. It's more like a second bedroom.[94] And still she's not satisfied. It's only when she stops looking outward and starts looking inward that she achieves anything like enlightenment.

This is all to say that when companies appeal to our nostalgic feelings about this movie, we can and should be wary of their motivations. There's a massive difference between the fantasy they're selling and the paltry reality of what we're buying. As *Clueless* enjoys its 30th anniversary and the tie-in merch piles up, we'd do well to remember that the original movie pokes fun at Cher's materialistic side — and her limited point of view, too. Because that's another thing about nostalgia: It's not the full picture.

If we continue to invite this movie into our lives, let's do so in ways that stay true to its actual messages — the ones it intends and the ones it makes without realizing. *Clueless* is, all at once, a sharp comedy about privilege, an unwitting indictment of color-blind approaches to race, a buoyant celebration of love and femininity, a poisonous enforcement of the classed world

---

94 The "closet" was filmed in a pool house, if that helps give you a sense of its actual size.

order, a hopeful meditation on community building, and a great movie to watch if you want to be entertained and challenged in one fell swoop. One thing this film definitely isn't: encouragement to shop 'til you drop. *Clueless* asks us to think, to laugh, to look inward and outward, to work together, to build something better.

Amy Heckerling's sweet comedy tries to imagine a more perfect world by modeling how one individual can do their part to help create a kinder society. Of course, as I've written throughout this book, major elements in *Clueless*'s vision of an improved social world fall flat — and yet, I think it would be shortsighted to dismiss the entire film for its flaws. At the end of the day, this movie is a good-hearted, insightful, and generative effort to chart a course beyond our sublunary world. It's a counternarrative to nihilism, a refusal to let cynicism, hopelessness, and passivity rule the day. For this alone, Heckerling deserves immense credit.[95]

Granted, all this may say more about me than the movie. I was diagnosed with clinical depression when I was a teenager (Cher's age, funnily enough), which is almost certainly part of why, when I think about the world and my place in it, I default

---

95  My language here is influenced by the critic Mark Fisher's excellent short essay on the film *Catching Fire* (2013). Relevant info: Fisher's work trenchantly critiqued capitalism for many years but, as he himself admitted, often struggled to do more than describe the apparently enclosed and unchangeable system in which we're trapped. Four years after his influential monograph *Capitalist Realism: Is There No Alternative?* (2008) seemingly answered its own subtitle with a resounding no, he published an awestruck essay in praise of Suzanne Collins's *Hunger Games* series and its cinematic adaptations. For Fisher, these young adult novels by a woman and about a young girl did nothing less than imagine a "counter-narrative to capitalist realism." Collins's oeuvre is a tremendous example of how allegedly low, feminine-coded art can generate revolutionary alternatives where more (scare quotes) "intellectual" criticism fails to do more than reiterate problems.

to feeling trapped in a hostile system's unceasing, vicious rule. For me, it's all too easy to get stuck in a dystopic frame of mind — to feel paralyzed by life's hardships and the world's banal, horrendous cruelties.

Beyond all the reasons outlined way back in chapter one, this may be the origin story of why I dislike gritty, dramatic films about tormented men so much. Most of the time, they're just not revelatory or interesting to me. Like, yes, the main character is sad because he understands that the world is terrible, and that life is characterized by pain. At certain periods in my life, I have felt that way — sometimes for years on end. What exactly is artistic or compelling about such an obvious, despondent outlook? After all, it doesn't give us new information: Most people already know that the world is horribly imperfect. But then again, this presupposes the idea that this kind of art wants to shift the dial — in actuality, I think movies like *Fight Club* (1999) and *Joker* (2019) are far more invested in reiterating the genius of the person experiencing these sad, deep thoughts than improving our collective wellbeing.

If, as happens so often, taxonomizing problems is where social critique begins and ends, then we can all too easily end up in a feedback loop of despair. At its worst, reiterating our undeniably flawed world is the desultory *as if* that dismisses the mere possibility of betterment. At its best, catalogs of social ills are the necessary beginning of a conversation that ultimately produces something better — the *as if* that imagines otherwise. Of the two, I know which approach I prefer. We need to move forward.

This is why I'm most impressed by art that understands the world's problems and then does the hard work of imagining hospitable alternatives. If someone can hold these two things in their hand at once and decide to amplify goodness, I admire that decision on the deepest level. It's much more difficult to propose a utopia than reflect a dystopia. The fact that *Clueless* does this so effortlessly, so brightly, so sweetly is what moves me most about the film. Cher and her friends hide profundity in plain sight when they insist that improving our communities matters, that it's possible, and that it's joyous. For me, this movie is a sneaky rallying cry, a secret message that resistance isn't futile. It's necessary, and it can happen in the most unlikely places. My task as a viewer — and a human — is to chip in as best as I can.

# *Works Cited

Alexander, Michelle. *The New Jim Crow: Mass Incarceration in the Age of Colorblindness.* The New Press, 2010.

Angelou, Maya, and Oprah Winfrey. "Dr. Maya Angelou's Most Important Lessons | The Oprah Winfrey Show | Oprah Winfrey Network." YouTube, uploaded by OWN: Oprah Winfrey Network, February 25, 2015. https://www.youtube.com/watch?v=xcXdHD nKV2g.

Apfelbaum, Evan P., Michael I. Norton, and Samuel R. Sommers. "Racial Colorblindness: Emergence, Practice, and Implications." *Current Directions in Psychological Science* 21, no. 3 (June 2012): 205–209.

Austen, Jane. *Emma*. Penguin Classics, 2003.

Austen, Jane. *Jane Austen's Letters*. Edited by Deirdre Le Faye. Oxford University Press, 2011.

Austen, Jane. *Persuasion*. Penguin Classics, 2003.

Barthes, Roland. *Mythologies*. Translated by Annette Lavers. Farrar, Straus, and Giroux, 1972.

Bell, Keaton. "Alicia Silverstone on the Legacy of *Clueless*, 25 Years Later." *Vogue*, July 19, 2020. https://www.vogue.com/article/alicia-silverstone-clueless-25th-anniversary-interview.

Berry, David. *On Nostalgia*. Coach House, 2020.

"Black Female Voices: bell hooks and Melissa Harris-Perry." Vimeo, uploaded by The New School, November 8, 2013. https://livestream.com/thenewschool/blackfemalevoices.

Boyce Davies, Carole. "*12 Years a Slave* Fails to Represent Black Resistance to Enslavement." *The Guardian*, January 10, 2014. https://www.theguardian.com/world/2014/jan/10/12-years-a-slave-fails-to-show-resistence.

Carnevale, Fulvia, and John Kelsey. "Art of the Possible: An Interview with Jacques Rancière." *Artforum* 45, no. 7 (March 2007).

Chaney, Jen. *As If: The Oral History of Clueless as Told by Amy Heckerling, the Cast, and the Crew.* Touchstone, 2015.

Chesterton, G.K. "The Vote and the House." *All Things Considered.* Methurn and Co., 1913, pp. 34–41.

Clark, Larry, dir. *Kids.* Featuring Leo Fitzpatrick, Justin Pierce, Chloë Sevigny, and Rosario Dawson. Independent Pictures and The Guys Upstairs, 1995.

Critchley, Simon. *On Humour.* Routledge, 2002.

Cusk, Rachel. "Shakespeare's Sisters." *Coventry: Essays.* Picador, 2019, pp. 163–176.

Denby, David. "*Clueless.*" *New York Magazine*, August 7, 1995.

"Ditz." *Dictionary of American Family Names.* Edited by Patrick Hanks. Oxford University Press, 2003.

"Donald Faison Says 'Together We Can Abolish Racism.'" YouTube, uploaded by *The Kelly Clarkson Show*, June 12, 2020. https://www.youtube.com/watch?v=IyuB_7cdWYc.

Driscoll, Catherine. *Teen Film: An Introduction.* Berg, 2011.

Ebert, Roger. "*Clueless.*" *Chicago Sun-Times*, July 19, 1995.

Empson, William. *Some Versions of Pastoral: A Study of Pastoral Form in Literature.* New Directions, 1950.

Epstein, Rebecca, Jamilia J. Blake, and Thalia González. "Girlhood Interrupted: The Erasure of Black Girls' Childhood." *Georgetown Law Center on Poverty and Inequality*, June 27, 2017.

Fisher, Mark. "Remember Who the Enemy Is." *K-Punk: The Collected and Unpublished Writings of Mark Fisher.* Edited by Darren Ambrose. Watkins Media, 2018, pp. 227–230.

Frye, Northrop. "Archetypal Criticism: Theory of Myths." *Anatomy of Criticism: Four Essays.* Princeton University Press, 1957, pp. 131–239.

Gleiberman, Owen. "*Clueless.*" *Entertainment Weekly*, July 28, 1995.

Gerwig, Greta, dir. *Lady Bird.* Featuring Saoirse Ronan, Laurie Metcalfe, Beanie Feldstein, Lucas Hedges, and Timothée Chalamet. A24, Universal Pictures, and Focus Features, 2017.

Gruen, Hannah, and Diana Beninati. "Cher from *Clueless* Was Totally Lesbian-Coded." *Her Campus*, October 23, 2018. https://www.hercampus.com/school/bryn-mawr/cher-clueless-was-totally-lesbian-coded/.

Halberstam, Jack. "Dude, Where's My Phallus? Forgetting, Looping, Losing." *The Queer Art of Failure*. Duke University Press, 2011, pp. 53–86.

Hamer, Fannie Lou. "Nobody's Free Until Everybody's Free." *The Speeches of Fannie Lou Hamer: To Tell It Like It Is*. Edited by Maegan Parker Brooks and Davis W. Houk. Oxford University Press, 2010, pp. 134–139.

Harris, Aisha. "Ebony and Ivory." *Wannabe: Reckonings with the Pop Culture That Shapes Me*. HarperCollins, 2023, pp. 125–158.

Hartman, Saidiya. *Lose Your Mother: A Journey Along the Atlantic Slave Route*. Macmillan, 2008.

Heckerling, Amy, creator. *Clueless*. Featuring Rachel Blanchard, Stacey Dash, Donald Faison, Elisa Donovan, and Sean Holland. Cockamamie Productions and Paramount Network Television Productions, 1996–1999.

Heckerling, Amy, dir. *Clueless*. Featuring Alicia Silverstone, Stacey Dash, Brittany Murphy, Paul Rudd, and Donald Faison. Paramount Pictures, 1995.

Heckerling, Amy. *Clueless* (original screenplay). ScreenCraft, August 1994. https://screencraft.org/wp-content/uploads/2019/11/Clueless.pdf.

Hong, Cathy Park. "The End of White Innocence." *Minor Feelings: An Asian American Reckoning*. One World, 2020, pp. 66–90.

hooks, bell. *All About Love: New Visions*. William Morrow, 2000.

Hu, Jane. "*Clueless* Is Still the Best Jane Austen Adaptation." *The Ringer*, July 17, 2020. https://www.theringer.com/movies/2020/7/17/21327905/clueless-jane-austen-adaptations.

Jefferson, Margo. *Constructing a Nervous System: A Memoir*. Vintage, 2022.

Johnson, Claudia L. "*Emma*: 'Woman, Lovely Woman, Reigns Alone.'" *Jane Austen: Women, Politics, and the Novel*. University of Chicago Press, 1988, pp. 121–143.

Keymer, Tom. "*Emma* and Englishness." *Jane Austen: Writing, Society, Politics*. Oxford University Press, 2020, pp. 107–125.

Koski, Genevieve. "*Clueless*' Big Confidence Sells Its Small Stakes." *The Dissolve*, April 8, 2014. https://thedissolve.com/features/movie-of-the-week/500-clueless-big-confidence-sells-its-small-stakes/.

Lethem, Jonathan. *They Live: A Novel Approach to Cinema*. Counterpoint, 2010.

Litman, Juliet, Amanda Dobbins, and K. Austin Collins, hosts. *The Rewatchables* podcast, "*Clueless*." The Ringer Podcast Network, October 5, 2017.

Lorde, Audre. *Sister Outsider: Essays and Speeches*. Crossing Press, 1984.

Mandell, Andrea. "Stacey Dash Tells Women to 'Work Harder.'" *USA Today*. April 29, 2015. https://www.usatoday.com/story/life/people/2015/04/29/stacey-dash-meredith-viera-gender-pay-gap/26593239/.

Maslow, Nick. "Stacey Dash Defends Her Oscars Joke: 'We Need to Stop Complaining About White People Oppressing Us.'" *People*. February 28, 2016. https://people.com /awards/oscars-2016-stacey-dash-explains-joke-with-chris-rock/.

McMillan Cottom, Tressie. "Black Girlhood, Interrupted." *Thick: And Other Essays*. The New Press, 2019.

Mallon, Thomas, and Pankaj Mishra. "Highbrow, Lowbrow, Middlebrow — Do These Kinds of Cultural Categories Mean Anything Anymore?" *The New York Times*, July 29, 2014. https://www.nytimes.com/2014/08/03/books/review/highbrow-lowbrow-middlebrow -do-these-kinds-of-cultural-categories-mean-anything-anymore.html.

Maslin, Janet. "Film Review; A Teen-Ager Who's Clear on Her Priorities." *The New York Times*, July 19, 1995. https://www.nytimes.com/1995/07/19/movies/film-review-a-teen -ager-who-s-clear-on-her-priorities.html.

Miller, Claire Cain. "As Women Take Over a Male-Dominated Field, the Pay Drops." *The New York Times*, March 18, 2016. https://www.nytimes.com/2016/03/20/upshot /as-women-take-over-a-male-dominated-field-the-pay-drops.html.

Mills, Alyssa. "Cher from *Clueless* Was Definitely a Lesbian — Here's Why." *An Injustice!* Medium, June 9, 2021. https://aninjusticemag.com/cher-from-clueless-was-definitely-a -lesbian-heres-why-efb75d24e256.

Morton, Samuel George. *CCrania Americana; Or, A Comparative View of the Skulls of Various Aboriginal Nations of North and South America: To Which Is Prefixed an Essay on the Varieties of the Human Species*. Simpkin, Marshall, and Co., 1839.

Nussbaum, Emily. *I Like to Watch: Arguing My Way Through the TV Revolution*. Random House, 2019.

Odell, Jenny. "Ecology of Strangers." *How to Do Nothing: Resisting the Attention Economy*. Melville House, 2019, pp. 127–154.

Orwell, George. *Essays*. Penguin, 2000.

Plett, Casey. *On Community*. Biblioasis, 2023.

Pride, Christine. "An Essay on the Importance of Interracial Friendships." *PBS News Hour*. October 19, 2020. https://www.youtube.com/watch?v=16g_LczFUA8.

Respers France, Lisa. "Stacey Dash: Transgender People Should Use Bushes for Bathrooms." CNN. June 2, 2016. https://www.cnn.com/2016/06/02/entertainment/stacey-dash-book -transgender-guns/index.html.

Rogers, Matt, host. Louis Virtel, guest. *HBO Max Movie Club* podcast, "*Clueless*." HBO Max. November 22, 2021.

Rogers, Matt, and Bowen Yang, hosts. Wendy Osefo, guest. *Las Culturistas* podcast, "Address Her Correctly!" Big Money Players, November 24, 2021.

Rogers, Matt, and Bowen Yang, hosts. Ziwe, guest. *Las Culturistas* podcast, "The Martin Luther King of Alt Comedy." Big Money Players, August 19, 2020.

Rowe, Kathleen. *The Unruly Woman: Gender and the Genres of Laughter.* University of Texas Press, 1995.

Silverstone, Alicia. *The Kind Mama: A Simple Guide to Supercharged Fertility, a Radiant Pregnancy, a Sweeter Birth, and a Healthier, More Beautiful Beginning.* Rodale Books, 2014.

Simone, Gail. "Character List." *Women in Refrigerators.* March 1999. https://www.lby3.com/wir/.

Slone, Isabel. "A Fossil of Our Youth: An Interview with Marlowe Granados." *Hazlitt,* November 24, 2020. https://hazlitt.net/feature/fossil-our-youth-interview-marlowe-granados.

Smith, Mychal Denzel. *Invisible Man, Got the Whole World Watching: A Young Black Man's Education.* Nation, 2016.

Smith, Zadie. *Changing My Mind: Occasional Essays.* Penguin, 2009.

"Special Featurettes." *Clueless: "Whatever" Edition*, DVD. Featuring Twink Caplan, Stacey Dash, Donald Faison, Amy Heckerling, Brittany Murphy, Paul Rudd, and Wallace Shawn. Paramount Pictures, 2005.

Speed, Lesley. *Clueless: American Youth in the '90s.* Routledge, 2017.

Srinivasan, Amia. "Coda: The Politics of Desire." *The Right to Sex: Feminism in the Twenty-First Century.* Picador, 2021, pp. 93–122.

Tallerico, Brian. "*The Falcon and the Winter Soldier* Recap: Front Line." *Vulture,* April 9, 2021. https://www.vulture.com/article/the-falcon-and-the-winter-soldier-episode-4-recap -the-whole-world-is-watching.html.

Thompson, Ayanna. *Blackface.* Bloomsbury Academic, 2021.

Thorne, Tara. "Low Road Forever." *Low Road Forever: And Other Essays.* Nimbus, 2022, pp. 188–195.

Tolentino, Jia. "Always Be Optimizing." *Trick Mirror: Reflections on Self-Delusion.* Random House, 2019, pp. 63–94.

Travers, Peter. "*Clueless.*" *Rolling Stone,* July 19, 1995. https://www.rollingstone.com/tv-movies /tv-movie-reviews/clueless-128551/.

White, Armond. "Dud of the Week; *12 Years a Slave* Reviewed by Armond White for *CityArts.*" New York Film Critics Circle. October 16, 2013. https://www.nyfcc.com/2013/10/3450/.

Wilson, Carl. *Let's Talk About Love: A Journey to the End of Taste.* Continuum, 2011.

Woloch, Alex. *The One vs. the Many: Minor Characters and the Space of the Protagonist in the Novel.* Princeton University Press, 2004.

Woolf, Virginia. *A Room of One's Own.* Penguin, 2020.

Zibrak, Arielle. *Guilty Pleasures.* New York University Press, 2021.

# *Works Consulted

Berger, John. *Ways of Seeing.* British Broadcasting Corporation and Penguin Books, 1972.

Cusk, Rachel. "*Eat, Pray, Love.*" *Coventry: Essays.* Picador, 2019, pp. 226–233.

Dash, Stacey. *There Goes My Social Life: From Clueless to Conservative.* Regnery, 2016.

Driscoll, Catherine. *Girls: Feminine Adolescence in Popular Culture and Cultural Theory.* Columbia University Press, 2002.

Dundas, Deborah. *On Class.* Biblioasis, 2023.

Fisher, Mark. *Capitalist Realism: Is There No Alternative?* Zero Books, 2009.

Gates, Henry Louis, Jr. *Loose Canons: Notes on the Culture Wars.* Oxford University Press, 1994.

Granados, Marlowe. "The Bimbo's Laugh." *The Baffler* 58. July 2021.

Granados, Marlowe. *Happy Hour.* Verso, 2021.

Kael, Pauline, and Andrew Davis. *Afterglow: A Last Conversation with Pauline Kael.* De Capo, 2003.

Laban, Monique. "Most Horrifying Happily Ever After: *Kate and Leopold* (2001)." *RomCom Superlatives: An Avidly Special Series.* Edited by Sarah Blackwood, Stephanie Hershinow, and Sarah Mesle. December 14, 2023.

Lee, Jen Sookfong. *Gentlemen of the Shade. My Own Private Idaho.* ECW, 2017.

Luse, Brittany, host. *It's Been a Minute* podcast, "Why We All Need a Himbo with *The Other Two*'s Josh Segarra." NPR, June 23, 2023.

McGurl, Mark. *The Novel Art: Elevations of American Fiction After Henry James*. Princeton University Press, 2001.

Nelson, Maggie. *On Freedom: Four Songs of Care and Constraint*. McClelland & Stewart, 2021.

Radway, Janice. *Reading the Romance: Women, Patriarchy, and Popular Culture*. University of North Carolina Press, 1984.

Showler, Suzannah. *Most Dramatic Ever. The Bachelor*. ECW, 2018.

Stearns, Peter N. *American Cool: Constructing a Twentieth-Century Emotional Style*. New York University Press, 1994.

Winant, Johanna. "Best Longing Look: *Clueless* (1995)." *RomCom Superlatives: An Avidly Special Series*. Edited by Sarah Blackwood, Stephanie Hershinow, and Sarah Mesle. December 14, 2023.

## Acknowledgments

This little book was a long time coming. It's only here because, for many years, I had the privilege of learning alongside clever, lovely people. To everyone — friends, family, colleagues, classmates, academic mentors — who tolerated my many questions about femininity, ethics, and media over the years, thank you for your time and consideration. My mom and dad fielded a lot of this; thinking about their lifelong enthusiastic encouragement of basically anything I do, no matter how nonsensical, makes me a little teary. Funny, insightful Charlie Barber unearthed the promising parts of an otherwise disastrous version of chapter two and chatted with me about community on a long wander through Winnipeg. Brilliant, warm Katherine Shwetz casually said it was important to celebrate "the love that is freely given" and changed my world. For the last decade, silly, perfect Mitch Johnston has shown me how the ideas in chapter four feel (i.e. very nice). He also watched *Clueless* with me many times, suggested consistently great sources, and bolstered me with snacks and compliments throughout the writing of this book. Charlie, Kash, and Mitch also read drafts of this book and gave me thoughtful, helpful feedback. Thanks, guys, you're the best! I also have to mention my sweet baby angel cats, Crumbs and Hodge, who make every day funnier and better. Further shout-outs go to my in-laws Alyson and Wayne (thank you for bearing with me) and my buds, especially Joan, Rasa, and Valerie, for cheering me on like a chorus of peppy angels.

I had never written a book before and didn't know if the experience would prove all those tortured artist narratives right. Thanks to my supportive, incisive editor Jen Sookfong Lee and the entire dream team at ECW Press, it did not. In the background of this project's surprising smoothness, I want to highlight my doctoral committee — Simon Dickie, Tom Keymer, and Terry Robinson — at the University of Toronto and my colleagues at Cape Breton University's English Department. I wrote this book while working at CBU and, in so many ways, it is only here because of this job. Having time to research, write, and edit is a precious gift. I also thank my past editor (now friend!) Dancy Mason, who helped me meld research with zippy writing at the beginning of my career. Related, earlier versions of material in chapters one and four, as well as the interlude on rom-com heroines making bad choices, were originally published in editorials for Factinate.com. I am grateful to Dancy Mason, the editor-in-chief, for permission to reprint these materials in this book.

Most of all, this wee book is for my big sister, Shannon Litt, an absolute sunbeam of a person. Shannon is the funniest, kindest, smartest, most big-hearted, silly human. I don't know what I did to clinch history's most advantageous genetic trade-off in which I landed her and she, poor thing, got stuck dealing with me. I love you, Shanny!

**Veronica Litt** is a reader, teacher, and hobbyist letterpress printer from southern Ontario. She holds a PhD in English and Book History from the University of Toronto, where her research concentrated on 18th-century novels. Veronica calls Hamilton home, though she currently lives and works in Nova Scotia teaching post-secondary classes on English literature. *Ugh! As If!* is her first book.

## Entertainment. Writing. Culture. ───────────

ECW is a proudly independent, Canadian-owned book publisher. We know great writing can improve people's lives, and we're passionate about sharing original, exciting, and insightful writing across genres.

──────────── **Thanks for reading along!**

We want our books not just to sustain our imaginations, but to help construct a healthier, more just world, and so we've become a certified B Corporation, meaning we meet a high standard of social and environmental responsibility — and we're going to keep aiming higher. We believe books can drive change, but the way we make them can too.

Being a B Corp means that the act of publishing this book should be a force for good — for the planet, for our communities, and for the people that worked to make this book. For example, everyone who worked on this book was paid at least a living wage. You can learn more at the Ontario Living Wage Network.

This book is also available as a Global Certified Accessible™ (GCA) ebook. ECW Press's ebooks are screen reader friendly and are built to meet the needs of those who are unable to read standard print due to blindness, low vision, dyslexia, or a physical disability.

The interior of this book is printed on Sustana EnviroBook™, which is made from 100% recycled fibres and processed chlorine-free.

FSC
www.fsc.org
MIX
Paper | Supporting responsible forestry
FSC® C016245

ECW's office is situated on land that was the traditional territory of many nations, including the Wendat, the Anishinaabeg, Haudenosaunee, Chippewa, Métis, and current treaty holders the Mississaugas of the Credit. In the 1880s, the land was developed as part of a growing community around St. Matthew's Anglican and other churches. Starting in the 1950s, our neighbourhood was transformed by immigrants fleeing the Vietnam War and Chinese Canadians dispossessed by the building of Nathan Phillips Square and the subsequent rise in real estate value in other Chinatowns. We are grateful to those who cared for the land before us and are proud to be working amidst this mix of cultures.